Women
of
Commitment

Personal Portraits
of Selected BYU Women

Women
of
Commitment

Personal Portraits
of Selected BYU Women

Compiled by
Marian Wilkinson Jensen

First Printing: July 1997

International Standard Book Number:

0-88290-610-0

Horizon Publishers' Catalog and Order Number:

1081

Printed and distributed
in the United States of America by

& Distributors, Incorporated

Mailing Address:
P.O. Box 490
Bountiful, Utah 84011-0490

Street Address:
50 South 500 West
Bountiful, Utah 84010

Local Phone: (801) 295-9451
WATS (toll free): 1 (800) 453-0812
FAX: (801) 295-0196

Internet: www.horizonpublishers.com

Contents

College of Nursing

College of Physical Education

Counseling Center

Library

Missionary Training Center

International Folk Dancers

Program Bureau, Young Ambassadors and Lamanite Generation

Friend and Supporter

Acknowledgments

My sincere appreciation to the many people who have contributed to this book. Ron Hyde, Vice-President of Advancement at Brigham Young University, gave me the go-ahead. He also enlisted the support of George Bowie, Assistant Vice-President of University Relations and Director of the Alumni Association. Scott Duvall and Mark Smith, research historians, also gave me assistance. And, of course, those who wrote the biographical sketches are the real authors.

My most constant encourager for the project has been my long-time friend, Shirley Wilkes Thomas. Others who gave encouragement, suggestions, and editorial aid include David Whittaker, Carrie Jenkins, Jan Nelson Ekeroth, Dr. Carol Cornwall Madsen, Dr. Mae Blanch, Mary Louise Seamons, Lisa Hawkins, Ellen Riddle, Joy Rigby, Nancy Jane Hamberlin, Ida Smith, Barbara Markham Daines, LaNedra King, Irva Andrus, Bonnie Ballif-Spanvill, Sharon Dawson, Brandon Miller, Genevieve Taylor-Oliver, Janette Jeffress, and Amy Leaver. And Dr. Marjorie Wight, a BYU English professor for many years, made many appropriate changes. Special thanks go to Linda Hunter Adams, director of the BYU Humanities Publications Center, who enlisted help from the students in her editing class and provided valuable resources and facilities. Helen Dixon completed the editing process and prepared the entire manuscript for publication.

Thanks also to my computer specialist par excellence, Marilyn Marley, who deciphered my often hard-to-read notes. Others assisting in this task were Allison Yauney, Phyllis Jensen, Stephanie DeGraff, Nisa Allred, and Janelle Riley.

My deceased husband, Gordon, a former faculty member at the University of Utah, was patient when I spent long hours on this project and was always understanding about my BYU loyalties, even paying for our daughters' tuition when they chose to attend "my school." Thanks and love must also go to our daughters, Susan, Elisabeth, and Allyson, who give purpose, direction, and joy to our lives.

Preface

*A*ccording to legend, when Brigham Young asked Dr. Karl G. Maeser to establish a Church academy in the frontier community of Provo, Brother Maeser remained quiet for a moment. Brigham Young, in his humorous but firm way, then said, "Brother Maeser, you can go to Provo, or you can go to hell." Obediently, Brother Maeser accepted the call, and his wife, Anna, accompanied him.

Anna Maeser was the predecessor of many women who have helped build this small academy of twenty-nine individuals to a bulging university student body of over 25,000 students. Brother Maeser once related a vision he had in which he saw hundreds of students and many large buildings of learning on "Temple Hill." Loyal and committed Anna Maeser worked beside her husband in making this vision come true. Many men and women joined their ranks. Alice Ludlow Wilkinson was one of them.

On August 6, 1983, my mother, Alice Wilkinson, passed away. Shortly after her passing, I wrote a short biographical sketch about her. It wasn't long before I felt the need to chronicle the lives of some of the other committed women who had been a part of her life while she presided as the "first lady" of Brigham Young University—women who had dedicated themselves to realizing Dr. Maeser's dream.

Compiling a list of such women became overwhelming. As the list grew, I knew I could select only a few to represent the many others. Then, as other, more current BYU women came to my attention, I knew I must bring my selection up-to-date. The result is a small sampling of women over several generations of BYU history. It doesn't begin to include all the worthy women at BYU—past and present—and the many fields they represent, but at least it is a beginning.

In some cases, the women I chose were those I knew best or of whom I was most aware. My hope is that the reader will have understanding for the many women not represented here, but will delight in those that are.

I wanted to include women who have conducted their lives in harmony with the gospel of Jesus Christ; who have been role models for the women students on campus; and who are unselfish, industrious, persistent, loyal, and intelligent. I have also tried to show that many great women, working in harmony with the great men of this university, have made significant contributions to BYU and the lives of others.

Whenever possible I selected a family member or close associate to write these biographical sketches. Thus, the authors generally wrote not only of the contributions these women made to the university, but also of the contributions they made to their families and friends. This book is a tribute to these women. I believe readers will derive inspiration from the lives of these women of great commitment.

BYU Women

The Women's Community

by

Helen Dixon, Ellen Powley, Muriel Thole, and Marian W. Jensen

The authors' memories have provided some of the details for this historical sketch, but much of the information has been taken from the minutes and yearbooks of this organization's archives.

*B*efore its official organization on December 18, 1917, BYU Women, a group of women from the BYU community, was already evolving. Delia Maeser, Susa Young Gates, and Zina Young Card were among the first to begin arranging faculty social activities. Then, under BYU President Benjamin Cluff, a little group calling itself the Sunshine Club was formed. From there, President George H. Brimhall called together a committee of BYU women to organize social activities for faculty members and their partners. From the minutes of this committee's meetings, beginning in 1914, we read:

"The matrons of the school entertained at Mrs. Jesse Knight's. Her beautiful home was opened to the guests and a most splendid afternoon was the result."

And in another place:

"At Merline Roylance's each lady was dressed to represent a book. The details were interestingly and charmingly worked out. A prize was awarded to Elizabeth Lindsay for the best representation, her book being *Keeping Up with Lizzie*."

In 1916, the organization elected a president and secretary, an action that finally led to President Brimhall's more permanent organization of the group in 1917, the name of BYU Women, and an adoption of official rules and regulations. Mrs. Christian Jensen was the first president of the seventy-five original members. The twofold objective of this early organization has remained in place to this day: (1) to provide intellectual and social opportunities for its members, and (2) to uphold and promote the ideals of the university.

For one of BYU Women's first activities, Maud May Babcock presented two dramatic reading recitals; the proceeds were then used to help furnish the "Art Room" on campus. The women also sent a telegram to a Utah senator, urging him to support the Women's Suffrage movement. Other events included musical renditions, a talk on the Red Cross, and food prepared by the university's "Domestic Science" class.

The first world war had its effects on the organization. Before 1918, BYU Women had contributed $125 to the Red Cross for "Belgian Relief." During 1918–19, meetings were curtailed by a flu epidemic, but officers encouraged the women to stay involved by feeding and collecting bedding for soldiers stationed in the area who were suffering from the flu. Political activity continued with the organization's 1920 telegrams to two senators urging them to support the League of Nations. And in an effort to uphold moral standards, the women discussed the censoring of picture shows to aid in crime prevention. (Have things changed so much?)

Beginning at this time, and extending over a period of many years, BYU Women welcomed the female students at a reception at the beginning of the year. At first this welcome included all the girls, but, as the student body increased in size, it had to be limited to the freshman girls.

The year 1921 was especially productive. It marked the beginning of the organization's publication of an annual yearbook. The women also began a long-standing program to promote and sponsor the Utah County Art Exhibit in Springville, Utah. A feature of this program was an activity in which the participants enjoyed a dinner in

Springville, followed by a tour of the exhibit. During this year, the organization also had a petition granted by the president of the university to permit members of BYU Women to attend classes on campus tuition free—a privilege that extended over a number of years. And finally, 1921 marked the beginning of the Memorial Library Project, through which many hundreds of books have been contributed to the BYU Library.

During the second world war, the group participated again in the war effort. Programs often featured discussions of war-related problems, and, as a result of a BYU Women-sponsored drive in 1943, members purchased $4,175 in war bonds. The group's officers debated about whether or not to continue serving refreshments at meetings because they were having difficulty finding enough nonrationed food. But they voted to continue as long as possible, and they proved themselves equal to the task. The minutes during this era also note that one night the police interrupted a social at the Joseph Smith Ballroom to see if everything was in order.

During the 1940s, BYU Women initiated a series of Sunday-evening fireside chats for members and guests. But the organization's main focus during this decade was to help the many new women joining the campus. They developed a newcomers program, which has been so successful that it still operates today. Handout information is prepared to help new families adjust to campus life and find local doctors, dentists, schools, and stores. And special activities help newcomers become acquainted with the community and meet other families.

In 1947, BYU Women meetings and socials centered around the centennial of the Mormon pioneers' arrival in Utah. The September 1950 social commemorated BYU's 75th anniversary, and the April 1951 meeting featured a tour of the new Eyring Science Center on campus. In February of 1951, the group welcomed Alice L. Wilkinson, wife of the new president, Ernest L. Wilkinson, in a "tea." Alice remembered how women faculty members prepared for her family's arrival by putting clean sheets and blankets on the beds in the President's Home—a welcome relief after their cold and harrowing drive from Washington, D.C. to Provo in the snow.

The university's expansion during the 1950s and 1960s prompted the administration, in 1959, to request that BYU Women open its membership to not only faculty members and faculty wives, but also to full-time staff members and staff wives. This important inclusion has helped to expand the organization's influence and promote the sisterhood that prompted Muriel Thole, the 1978–79 president, to say that, whether the women be presidents' and deans' wives, the wives of cooks and custodians, or women faculty and staff members, they "all stand under the same umbrella: BYU Women."

Muriel Thole provides some favorite memories from her many years with BYU Women that give insight into the sisterhood and enjoyment cultivated by the organization. During an athletic event once, the BYU Women entertained the wives of the coaches attending from other schools. They visited some of the area's mountains and canyons and then went to Temple Square. Later in the day, they returned to campus to attend a fashion show in which BYU students served as the models. The visiting women were impressed by the beautiful, well-dressed students. When the girls announced the cost of their outfits, all purchased at Deseret Industries, the visitors were both amazed and delighted.

In the autumn of 1971, BYU Women planned to welcome BYU's new "first lady," June Oaks, during their first meeting of the year. To help the women become acquainted with her, the organizers invited June to be a greeter. Muriel Thole was delighted to be the other greeter and bought a new dress for the occasion. But her delight was extinguished when she saw June arrive wearing the same dress. June's comment, "I see we both have great taste," changed what could have been an embarrassing situation to a humorous one.

Over the years, BYU Women have worn many hats. Volunteers have helped at homeless and abused shelters, hosted athletic and cultural events, and served on boards for special events. For a while, some BYU Women were "pink ladies" at the McDonald Health Center, which provides students with medical care.

The organization has sponsored a number of projects that have benefited both university and community. On campus, BYU Women have made substantial contributions to the Endowment Fund, the Department of Family Sciences, the old BYU Training School playground, the art collections, and toward the purchase of items like pianos and band uniforms. And, often, when a monetary surplus is found, the organization offers student scholarships. But the group's service has extended well beyond the confines of the university as BYU Women have contributed to such diverse causes as the Belgian and British Relief Funds (during wartime), the Red Cross, the Polio Foundation, and the Utah Valley Regional Medical Center.

Although BYU Women enjoy getting together for social reasons, it was their distinguished history and record of service that were the main causes for celebration during the 1992 BYU Women 75th Anniversary birthday party, held in the Skyroom of the Wilkinson Center on campus. Members enjoyed lunch, birthday cake, and more importantly, a presentation recounting the activities and caring gestures of BYU Women from the past. All the women agreed that this event went a long way toward keeping the enduring missions of this organization—to provide intellectual and social opportunity and to promote charity and the ideals of the university—alive and in mind for the future.

Alice Ludlow Wilkinson

by

Marian W. Jensen and Alice W. Anderson

As a schoolgirl, I always knew I could relate each day's experiences to my mother and she would listen with interest. She brought this same demeanor into her professional and social gatherings at BYU, where she never dominated, but instead, listened. I hope this biographical sketch will help you come to know the same Alice Wilkinson I knew.

—MWJ

*I*n 1984, Allyson Jensen, a BYU student body vice-president, was reading some student newspapers of yesteryear. A certain article caught her eye—a brief tribute to a BYU student of 1922. It reads as follows:

> Joyousness without boisterousness,
> Charm without frivolity
> Cordiality without patronage,
> Talent without vanity,
> Ability without intrusion
> Poise without hauteur
> Friendliness without gush,
> And all this means just Alice.

—BYU News, March 1922

Allyson wondered who this person was. She reread the tribute three more times, then with surprise realized she was reading about her own grandmother, Alice Ludlow Wilkinson. That night she relayed this finding to me, her mother, by telephone. I too was amazed at these few words that so eloquently described my mother's personality, and when I later read the tribute in print, I again marveled at the accuracy of the description. What is perhaps even more remarkable to me, though, is that the woman so described came from the somewhat humble beginnings she did.

After graduation from Spanish Fork High School, Alice Ludlow had important decisions to make. Her early years on the farm—with father and mother, grandfather, seven younger brothers and sister, and many uncles, aunts, and cousins—had been happy, but she knew farming could be hard and unpredictable. On occasion Alice helped her father and brothers with the farm work. But most of her after-school time was spent at home, helping with the housework: cooking daily meals on the family's coal stove, preparing huge meals for the threshers, and canning the harvest. In school she excelled scholastically and in drama. She even took the lead in several musical productions.

Nathaniel Ludlow had always been able to provide well for his family from his large garden, but he had little cash. So when it came time for Alice to go to college, he informed her that he would not be able to send her. She was crushed. After some hesitation, she pleaded her cause, promising that she would baby-sit or work in the canning factory during the summers. Nathaniel, touched by her earnestness, took her to the bank where he borrowed money for her education. And true to his word, he was able to pay back this loan within the promised year's time.

With that borrowed money, Alice began the course that would determine the rest of her life. She attended BYU by commuting twelve miles every day on the local Bamberger train—a ride that allowed her to meet many fellow students. During her three years on campus, Alice not only studied conscientiously, but also participated in plays produced by Dr. T. Earl Pardoe (*It Pays to Advertise* and *Clarence*, by Booth Tarkington) and other student-body events, many of which she recorded in her brief memoir. Among her favorites were Coach Eugene Robert's annual hike up Mt. Timpanogos, President George Brimhall's daily devotionals, and Florence Jepperson Madsen's musicals. And Robert Sauers's BYU Band frequently played the ever-popular "When It's Springtime in the Rockies." Alice loved to sing along on the BYU college song, and many years later at a BYU Alumni gathering, she was perhaps the only one in the group who remembered all the words, which she sang with enthusiasm.

The most frequent mentions in her memoir are of a young debater who was also editor of the school newspaper, Ernest Wilkinson. When she first met him she had no premonition of the part he would play in her life. She remembered:

> In my sophomore year I ran for the vice-president of the student body. The young man most responsible for my election was Ernest Wilkinson. He claimed that in trying to convince the students of my qualifications as a vice-president, he convinced himself of my qualifications as a wife.
>
> Three years after our introduction to one another, we were married in 1922 in the Salt Lake Temple. A few days later we were on our way to Washington, D.C., where Ernest was to enter George Washington Law School. We traveled in an ancient

Dodge car, packed to the roof with our earthly belongings, including some camping equipment (we could not afford the price of a motel). When we arrived, we had less than one dollar between us. Fortunately we were both able to get teaching jobs in the public school system.

During her marriage, Alice gave birth to five children—Ernest, Marian, Alice, David, and Douglas—and moved with her husband from Washington, D.C., to New Jersey, New York, and finally back to D.C. She wrote, "Those Washington, D.C., years were busy—Ernest had a demanding law practice and served in the stake presidency with both President Benson and, later, President J. Willard Marriott. And I was busy with a growing family." We children remember our years in Washington, D.C., vividly, perhaps because our mother had the most time to give us then.

She loved to sing and read to us. How well I remember her singing us some of the popular songs of her day—"Oh Johnny," "Our Grandfather's Clock," and "A Mormon Boy." And she read us the most delightful bedtime stories—*Wynkin, Blynkin, and Nod, The Sugarplum Tree*, and *The Little Engine That Could*. My mother was also a good seamstress. How I prized the Red-Riding-Hood cape she made for me one Halloween! And my sister, Alice Ann, and I still remember the twin princess-style dresses she sewed for us on her old treadle sewing machine.

Alice took her homemaking seriously—she was an especially good cook. Our Sunday-evening mealtime not only featured her excellent roasts, but was also often a time when our family relaxed and had fun. During these meals, Mother established a tradition of open family discussion. One of our favorite topics was our many friends and the Sunday activities in the Washington D.C., Chevy Chase Ward, where we went to church. Occasionally Mother would also tell a story, which she did well and with a twinkle in her eye.

Mother also supported her children in their many activities. For a short time our oldest brother played the trumpet, and mother endured the "jam sessions" at our home. My own advancement on the piano was largely a result of her encouragement. And throughout our growing up years, Alice was not only mother to us, but shared our home with others—on different occasions an aunt, an uncle, and our grandfather. But, along with all this activity and change were certain constants: our parents expected all the children to be obedient to the gospel and to be conscientious students.

Alice Wilkinson's service at home was also accompanied by consistent church service. She served as president of the Relief Society three different times. During World War II, I remember that the sisters of our Chevy Chase Ward gathered at the Wilkinson home to sew work shirts and overalls, which were then sent with other clothing and food items to the European saints. After twenty-five years of absence from this ward, I was able to pay a visit. I was impressed with how many people still remembered my mother. One sister, Leora Willey, mentioned that Mother had visited her in the hospital. A convert, Arlene Potter, said Mother had asked her to serve in her first important church assignment. And a single sister, Lillian, remembered her kindness. Alice's tact and graciousness were always mentioned.

These many years of giving served as a prelude to Alice Wilkinson's more public life. Her 1976 autobiographical sketch tells of the dramatic turn in her life:

> My husband was suddenly called by the First Presidency to serve as the president of BYU. The thought was overwhelming. In February 1951, we moved into the President's Home on the BYU campus. For twenty years it was our home.
>
> A burgeoning student body and a spectacular building program dominated these years, which were made memorable by sweet associations with eager young students and the General Authorities. There were, of course, trials and anxieties. My husband endured two massive heart attacks and open-heart surgery.

During his twenty-year tenure, my father gave the university everything he had. And backing him all the way was my mother. She listened to his concerns and acted as a sounding board for his many worries. She kept the home quiet and orderly and mingled and worked with the students, their parents, and the faculty members and spouses.

The late 1960s was a tense period for my parents. Over 1800 major universities in the United States were experiencing student demonstrations or uprisings, so my father felt he had to lead the university with a firm hand. He adamantly refused to permit the radical SDS organization (Students for a Democratic Society) to be established on campus. As a result, BYU was the only university unhindered by these violent uprisings in which buildings were demolished and at least one student was killed.

My father's firmness may have led to the saying bantered about on campus: "Let's go hear President Wilkinson's talk on the law of free-agency and how to enforce it." Both Mother and Dad loved humor, and they must have laughed at such comments. For underneath Dad's somewhat gruff exterior was a man sensitive to the needs and feelings of the students—he even gave generously of his own money to hundreds of needy students.

Over her years as "first lady," Alice acted as hostess for Sunday-evening student get-togethers at the President's Home. Her favorite menu for these occasions was hot spiced pineapple juice and cinnamon rolls. She also stood in line at receptions—frequently on the lawn of the President's Home—and greeted the parents of graduating students. On one such occasion, the caterers had undercalculated the amount of punch needed to serve the guests. In her practical way, she collected some cans of juice from our family's food storage, and no guest went away without something to drink.

Alice enjoyed meeting the Church Authorities and other dignitaries that visited the campus. The weekly devotional and forum addresses frequently featured a General Authority, including Presidents McKay, Lee, and Kimball, or distinguished people such as Cecil B. DeMille, Norman Thomas, Maria von Trapp, and Richard Nixon. Mother always provided such visitors with a genuine welcome.

In addition, Mother mingled with the students. On several occasions, worried students came to her privately to discuss personal concerns. Mother regarded these chats as confidential, and even today we do not know who these students were or what problems they faced.

Alice loved the university's cultural events. When dramas, concerts, or other special productions were presented on campus, she was almost always there, completely absorbed. My parents even acted as co-sponsors on one early trip to Europe with the then new International Folk Dancers.

The establishment of wards and stakes on campus was what my father and mother considered their most important contribution to BYU. In the mid 1950s my mother was asked to serve as the president of the first BYU Relief Society program. Relief Society was new to these girls, and Mother was aware of some skepticism in the Church regarding the appropriateness of Relief Society for them. But, the younger women on campus embraced the program with enthusiasm.

While serving in this capacity, Alice was called to be on the Relief Society General Board and soon found herself assigned to travel to foreign countries. She wrote of her experiences:

> During these trips two of us always traveled together with two members of the Primary General Board. In some of the countries there were serious problems, and even the mission presidents feared for us at times. But we were blessed with protection and an ability to travel freely from country to country.

As chair of the Relief Society Cultural Refinement Committee, Alice initiated the publication of the five volumes of *Out of the Best Books*, used by the Relief Society during this time. She enlisted the help of authors Bruce Clark and Robert Thomas and then reminded them of publication deadlines. When they failed to meet them, Alice would remind again. They responded to her prodding with good humor, even dedicating one of the books to Alice Wilkinson: "Our gracious prompter."

Alice's kindness and service endeared her to all she knew, but at times her own humor became her saving grace. A few anecdotes reveal her wit. When our father reiterated many times his desire to be buried in a pine box, she would retort, "For once, my dear Ernest, you'll have nothing to say!" Later in her life, on a shopping excursion with her daughter, Alice Ann, Mother was unable to decide between two dresses. She finally purchased both, exclaiming, "Your father will turn over in his grave!" Mother and daughter smiled at each other, agreeing, "That's all right, he'll just have to turn right back!" And finally, after leaving BYU, our dignified and usually conservative mother surprised us all. She needed a new car, and, at a time when most cars came in somber colors, she purchased a bright red Chevrolet on her own. She seemed to enjoy her "flashy" new automobile.

After a long twenty-year tenure at BYU, my father resigned as president in 1971. A friend, Norman Vincent Peale, wrote to him at the time: "Ernest, you will be like a fire engine trying to become a hearse." Mother and Dad laughed at this statement, but knew it was definitely time to retire. They then lived in Salt Lake City and spent winters in the milder climate of Palm Springs. During this period, Dad wrote his four-volume history of BYU. Mother read it, gave her suggestions, and, in contrast to my father's long four volumes, wrote an unpublished eight-page autobiographical sketch of her own life. Of her understanding and love of the gospel of Jesus Christ, she stated in this account, "I know of a certainty that it is true."

Dad's failing health and repeated heart attacks took his life in 1978. After that, Alice lived quietly, but continued to serve—specifically, on the committee that established the Belle S. Spafford chair in the Graduate School of Social Work at the University of Utah and on the board of the Utah Arthritis Foundation.

Still "hooked" on BYU athletics, Alice continued to tune in on the basketball and football games during these later years. Because of her keen interest in current events and politics and political figures, she also continued to read the morning newspaper—something she had always done. At times she would come to our home for Sunday dinners. Our daughters were in awe of her refinement, her willingness to listen, and her tasteful clothes. Little did they know that, because of her meager resources, her wardrobe during one year of college had consisted of a single reversible dress she had made herself.

Mother remained interested in her grandchildren to the end. For example, she corresponded with our daughter, Susan, who was a missionary in Chile, even after Mother's eyesight had grown increasingly dim. She also continued to participate in her grandchildren's important events. One spring morning in 1983, she dressed herself in her best clothes, including a new fur jacket (the only one she ever had), and drove herself to the chapel where her grandson, Christopher, was to be baptized. As she sat waiting for the ordinance, she suddenly experienced a cerebral stroke. After a two-month hospitalization, we finally took her home, where, on August 6, 1983, she quietly passed away. When we relayed the news to our missionary daughter in Chile, Susan's shock and sadness reiterated how we all felt. Sixteen years later, we still talk about my mother, miss her, and think of her magnificent example.

June Dixon Oaks

by

Sharmon Oaks Ward and Dallin D. Oaks

June Oaks could well have been the most high-spirited, fun-loving "first lady" of BYU. Her son, Dallin, and daughter, Sharmon, provide a delightful portrait of this woman and her service.

On returning to BYU in 1971 as the new president's wife, June Oaks observed, "The thing that astonished me most after our University of Chicago years was seeing all the expectant mothers at BYU. After nine years of waiting and wanting another child, I dared not dream that after four years at BYU I would be one of them." June Oaks was probably the only first lady of BYU to give birth to a child while living in the President's Home. During the centennial year (1975) each BYU department was asked to sponsor a significant event. To the Oaks family the 1975 birth of Jenny was their special centennial event.

Like her husband Dallin, June was born in Provo. On March 24, 1933, True Call and Charles H. Dixon of Spanish Fork became the parents of identical twin girls, Jean and June. Always inseparable, these twins tap-danced, played twin pianos, and performed with the BYU Program Bureau. Marrying after her first year at BYU, June delayed her education for children and her husband's schooling. Then, with much work and determination, she completed a B.S. degree from BYU in 1965—fourteen years after she entered as a freshman. To realize her dream of a BYU degree, June took her small children to Provo four times to enroll in summer school, completed home-study courses, and transferred credits to BYU from three different midwestern universities.

June has never lost her enthusiasm and vitality, which are manifest in simple ways, whether engaging in an animated conversation in an airport terminal, on the street, or in a grocery store, or breaking into spontaneous tap-dancing on her kitchen floor. Her energy seems boundless. She taught early-morning aerobics classes for several years, and for the past nine years has begun each day, Monday through Saturday, with a three-mile walk. When she was expecting her sixth child she played tennis until one week before the baby was born. She was grateful it rained that last week so she could stay home. She still plays tennis four times a week.

As the "first lady" of BYU for nine years (1971–80), June found herself in a new setting and role as she became involved in various receptions, hosting opportunities, and university functions. But she had qualities that endeared her to the BYU community. Besides being spontaneous and fun, she was genuine and "down-to-earth." The title or position a person held was not important to her. She was just as likely to take lemonade out to the lawn maintenance crew as to host guests in the President's Home.

At times June probably surprised people who had certain expectations of a "first lady." Some were surprised when the Oaks family brought their Great Dane, Gretchen, to live with them in the President's Home. That Great Dane became an unofficial mascot of sorts, being featured in cartoons in the campus newspaper, playing a role (at the students' request) in a student-sponsored assembly, and giving birth to a single pup June named "Cougar."

Imagine the surprise of one student who rang the doorbell of the President's Home and within moments found himself in a chair receiving a haircut. This student, the son of one of June's Chicago friends, had stopped by on another errand. Noticing his hair was in direct and conspicuous violation of BYU's dress and grooming standards, June good- naturedly coaxed him into an immediate and free haircut in the kitchen of the President's Home.

One of the traits that characterizes June Oaks is the strength and resolve that causes her to speak her mind without hesitation when convinced of the merit of her position or cause. As a Relief Society president living in Chicago, she received a call for help from a ward member who had just been beaten by her abusive husband. June went immediately, arriving at the woman's house after her husband had left. As June was assisting the woman, whose nose had been broken, the husband returned and was infuriated at finding that his wife had called for help. June stepped in front of the injured woman and rebuked her husband, saying, "You ought to be ashamed of yourself. No man has a right to beat a woman." June's courage and resolve were sufficient to the situation, and the man relented and let her attend to his wife's injuries and take her to the hospital.

On another occasion, after becoming the mother of several children and while pregnant with another, a Church member in Chicago asked June if she was "trying to populate the world all by herself." In typical forthright fashion, more to make a point about the inappropriateness of the question than to express any sort of personal philosophy, June responded, "I can't think of anyone better to do it."

June is resourceful and independent. She doesn't let a little trouble and work deter her from something worthwhile. If a piece of furniture in a second-hand store looked promising, she might buy it, repair it, and refinish it herself. She's been known to roll up her sleeves and try her hand at upholstery, electrical repairs, and plumbing. She is also adept at painting and wallpapering.

With her many skills and talents, June has given valuable service to her community, her church, and her family. She understands that service, while seldom convenient, pays rich dividends in joy. Her service has been richly varied. She is currently serving by appointment of the governor as a board member of the Utah Arts Council. She has spoken many times to university and church-sponsored programs and meetings, and to civic and community meetings as well. She has served as a board member of the Utah Symphony Guild, and as co-chair of the symphony's Outreach program in the public schools. She is a popular speaker, not just because she has a variety of experiences and insights to share, mingled with good common sense, but because she, herself, is interesting and is thus able to entertain, instruct, and edify, all at the same time.

Having been a ward Relief Society and Young Women president, as well as a teacher in the Primary, Relief Society and Sunday School, June has had many opportunities to serve others and make a difference in individual lives. But her service to individuals hasn't been limited to opportunities that have arisen within the context of Church assignments. In a quiet, unheralded way she has given friendship and assistance to countless others. For example, while in Chicago she welcomed a foreign student family into her home for a few weeks until the father could find a place for his family to live.

The greatest service June has provided is to her family of six children and twenty-three grandchildren. Her commitment to and love for her family have always been evident, and her sacrifices have helped to assure the success of each family member. She has always given the necessary time when it was important to any family member. At times this meant sharing her musical appreciation and talents, whether by practicing with the children or composing music for one of their programs. At other times it meant sewing late into the night to have someone's dress or costume ready the next day, helping type a paper just before it was due in a class, or rehearsing memorized lines with a child for an upcoming performance. She never hesitated to inconvenience herself when it meant providing meaningful experiences for her children. She has taken her children to music lessons, concerts, movies, plays, museums, parks, libraries, and zoos. Others were also included, such as when she, as YWMIA President, drove ward basketball teams to games in a stake that covered all of the southern and western suburbs of Chicago.

June is always interested in listening to her children. They recall how fun it was to talk to her after school and tell her about what had happened that day and about their frustrations and challenges. She would listen, encourage, or make suggestions. Even now, her children would rather be with her than with any of their own friends. Occasionally her suggestions weren't what her children wanted to hear, but they were the right thing. And sometimes they were just good for a laugh. If a child would complain, "Mom, it hurts when I bend my elbow," she would respond, "Then don't bend your elbow," or, "It will feel better when it stops hurting."

Her children all feel that they can discuss just about anything with her. She told them she felt that way about her own mother and was eager that her children feel the same way about her. She explained that when her young friends had questions about sensitive matters they would ask Jean and June to get the answer from their mother, and they did.

This same openness in communication aids in the closeness her family feels. Family members thoroughly enjoy each other's company. And when disagreements arise, they are expressed, resolved, and forgotten. June has continued to nourish this togetherness by welcoming her thirty-six-member family for countless dinners as often as distances allow. Visiting for hours around the dinner table is one of the great pleasures of all family members. Her home has always been a haven for family and friends.

June is protective of her children. The notoriety of her husband has brought a few unwelcome challenges. On one occasion a disgruntled and unstable man was threatening physical harm to one of the Oaks girls. A type of temporary police protection was offered to the family but BYU President Oaks declined, explaining that, in this case, his daughter probably didn't need the protection, but the man might need it if he tried anything while June was around.

June was strengthened by living sixteen years in and near the challenging neighborhoods of Chicago. One experience she'll never forget occurred when she and her husband drove an elderly sister home from a church meeting. Arriving at their destination in the dangerous neighborhood of the Blackstone Rangers gang on the south side of Chicago, Dallin walked the sister to her apartment while June remained in the locked car. As Dallin started back to the car he noticed three young men walking past. He cautiously waited until they were some distance away, and then quickly returned to the car. As he waited for June to unlock the door, both saw one of the men suddenly running back toward them. It was obvious to both June and Dallin that this man had a gun in his hand. Realizing she did not have time to unlock the car and admit her husband, June simply left the door locked and waited helplessly as the man confronted her husband at gunpoint.

As the young man held a gun against Dallin's stomach just outside the car window, June wondered what she should do. Should she honk the horn and try to get someone's attention? Should she drive away and try to find help? Or should she simply do nothing but watch the terrifying scene? She offered a silent prayer and had a peaceful feeling that everything would turn out all right. She knew she should do nothing, but her apprehensions remained.

After agonizing minutes while the robber repeatedly asked for money, which her husband did not have, and for the keys to the car, which he refused to give, the young man became very agitated and angry. He continued poking the gun in Dallin's stomach, repeating his demands for money and the car keys and adding, "Do it or I'll kill you." Again and again the demands were refused.

While watching this frightening scene from inside the car, June wondered, would she become a widow and have to raise five children alone, as her mother-in-law had done with her three small children?

But once again, June felt the influence of the Comforter and was reassured that all would be well.

After one last unsuccessful attempt to get money and car keys, the robber suddenly turned and ran back toward his companions. This ordeal had ended without loss of life or property. When June saw it was safe, she opened the car door and she and Dallin offered a prayer of gratitude that they had both been preserved.

When asked, "What is your greatest achievement?" June answers, "Our children." She has had six children by caesarean section and has accepted President David O. McKay's counsel that, "No success can compensate for failure in the home." Nurturing her family was June's profession. Joy now comes from seeing her children love and nurture their own children. Her children were taught that each generation should strive to build on the strengths, teachings, and experiences of past generations, while remaining steadfast in the Church.

June is committed to the Church and to the Lord. She has always encouraged her children to do what is right. She has provided a valuable example of how to support a spouse properly in church service. Once when one of her daughters began to complain about how much her own husband was gone because of church responsibilities, June explained how important it was to avoid such feelings. She has an unswerving testimony and commitment to the truths of the restored gospel of Jesus Christ.

32

Patricia Terry Holland

by

Mary Alice Holland McCann

Many students at BYU have rollicked with laughter at Patricia and Jeffrey Holland's humorous remarks in their joint devotional talks. To the students' delight, the Hollands sometimes told of their courtship. On September 5, 1981, Pat Holland related the following incident:

We really have a perfect marriage. My father told me we would have, even when we were just dating. Just a few nights before we were to be married, we had some kind of a little lovers' quarrel, and I was really upset with Jeff and said, "Please take me home." He brought me home and I ran into the house, slammed the door, ran into my father's bedroom, woke him up out of a dead sleep, and said, "Daddy, you've got to call this wedding off. This marriage just won't work."

My father in all his wisdom sat up in bed and said, "I will not call this marriage off. This marriage was made in heaven." When I stopped crying long enough to find out why, he said, "Because the rocks in Jeff's head will fill the holes in yours."[1]

Pat Holland's sense of humor is only one of her many fine attributes. This biographical sketch, by the Hollands' only daughter, Mary Alice, reveals more of her qualities, especially her love and faith.

*D*uring the summer of 1940, Marilla Terry Barlocker, then three months pregnant, was threatened with a miscarriage. Her doctor advised her to continue her normal activities and allow the seemingly inevitable miscarriage to occur. Determined to bear the child she already loved, Marilla called upon the faith that had seen her and her husband, Maeser Terry, through many challenges. She decided to confine herself to bed in what doctors called a futile attempt to keep her baby. She had to lie on her back in the tent that was temporarily serving as a home and entertain her two small sons while enduring the heat of southern Utah. Finally, on February 16, 1941, she gave birth to her first daughter, Patricia Terry.

The story of Patricia's birth is indicative of the faith and mettle of both her parents and their pioneer ancestors. Pat was born in Enterprise, Utah, where, in addition to attending school, she worked on the family farm alongside her brothers and in the small mercantile business her father owned. In her home she did regular chores, helped rear her younger brother, and practiced the piano several hours every day. Patricia's childhood activities represent the values by which she was raised: honesty, hard work, responsibility, integrity to one's talents, and an unconditional love of family. Her parents cultivated this love by teaching their children to live gospel principles and by making time to enjoy each other. Those who know Pat well have inevitably heard her recount childhood memories of riding horses bareback all over the countryside with her father, going camping with her brothers, and lying in the fields of tall grass with her cousins while they ate gooseberries and dreamed dreams.

Two of those dreams included meeting a handsome boy and someday living in a "big city," like nearby St. George. Those two dreams came true. When Patricia was nearing fifteen, her family moved to St. George, where she spent the remainder of her adolescent years. There she met Jeffrey R. Holland, who became enamored with Pat and, acting appropriately for a sixteen-year-old, teased her mercilessly until she vowed she would either have to marry him or never speak to him again. As years went by they began to date and, following Jeff's mission and Pat's year of musical training in New York, they were married in the St. George Temple on June 7, 1963.

When they first arrived at BYU, the school seemed overwhelming to them. Pat Holland says:

> The housing people were very helpful in providing lists of apartments. . . . The folks in the employment center suggested where we might work. We pieced together some furniture and found some friends. Then we splurged, left our new forty-five-dollar-a-month, two-room-and-a-shower apartment to have an evening meal in the Wilkinson Center cafeteria. We were impressed and exhilarated and still terrified.

Jeff continues:

> I remember one of those beautiful summer evenings walking up from our apartment on Third North and First East to the brow of the hill where the Maeser Building so majestically stands. Pat and I were arm in arm and very much in love, but school had not started, and there seemed to be so very much at stake. We were nameless, faceless, meaningless little undergraduates seeking our place in the sun. And we were newly married, each trusting our future so totally to the other, yet hardly aware of that at the time. I remember standing about halfway between the Maeser Building and the President's Home and being suddenly overwhelmed with the challenge I felt—new family, new life, new education, no money and no confidence. I remember turning to Pat and holding her in the beauty of that August evening and fighting back the

tears. I asked, "Do you think we can do it? Do you think we can compete with all these people in all these buildings who know so much more than we do and are so able? Do you think we've made a mistake?" Then I said, "Do you think we should withdraw and go home?"

... I guess that was the first time I saw what I would see again and again and again in her—the love, the confidence, the staying power, the reassurance, the careful handling of my fears and the sensitive nurturing of my faith, especially faith in myself. She (who must have been terrified herself, especially now, linked to me for life) nevertheless set aside her own doubts, slammed shut the hatch on the airplane and grabbed me by the safety belt. "Of course we can do it," she said. "Of course we're not going home." Then ... she gently reminded me that surely others were feeling the same thing, that what we had in our hearts was enough to get us through, that our Father in heaven would be helping.

And Pat adds:

If you stand on the south patio of the President's Home, you can see exactly the spot two vulnerable, frightened, newly married BYU students stood twenty-two years ago ... Some nights we stand and look out on that spot—usually nights when things have been a little challenging—and we remember those very special days.[2]

They did stay at BYU, succeeded admirably, and later moved to New Haven, Connecticut, where Jeffrey obtained his Ph.D. from Yale University.

During these years their family grew to include Matthew, Mary Alice, and David. In addition to bearing and rearing three children, Patricia fulfilled many church callings, including serving as a Relief Society president on four different occasions and in various Young Women and Primary callings. All of this training helped prepare her for the service she would render at Jeff's side when he was called in 1980 to serve as the president of Brigham Young University.

Between 1980 and 1989 Patricia served the faculty, staff, and especially the students of BYU, not only with her time but also with her heart. Her fervent prayers before her devotional addresses and firesides were not offered out of a fear of potential criticism, but out of a desire to help LDS students find peace and joy. In addition to fulfilling speaking engagements, Pat regularly hosted General Authorities, visiting dignitaries, and faculty in her home. Her efforts and her love for BYU were recognized in the winter of 1988 when she received the Exemplary Womanhood Award.

Toward the end of Jeff's tenure at BYU, Pat was called to serve as a counselor in the General Young Women presidency from 1984 to 1986, working together with Sisters Ardith Kapp and Maurine Turley. Although this calling exacted even more time from an already full schedule, Pat could still frequently be seen hugging students in the Marriott Center after basketball games, eating with students at the Cougareat, or walking and visiting with students on campus. As the years pass, Patricia will be honored for many contributions she made to BYU; however, the contribution for which she would most want to be remembered is that she loved the students. She wanted desperately for them to know that the Lord loved them and that if they lived the gospel all things would work together for their good.

Regardless of the service she performed outside the home, her children always knew that they were her first priority. While they can each remember many meetings their mother missed and speaking engagements that had to be cancelled, they find it nearly impossible to recall a single piano recital, basketball tournament, football game, cheerleading tryout, junior prom, or school play she ever missed. Many BYU students can attest to seeing her in the back yard of the President's Home throwing a football to David while he practiced his running pattern, or watching Mary practice her back handsprings, or standing under the backboard rebounding shots for Matthew. However, neither the BYU students nor those of the outside world will ever know the hours she spent reading to her children and rocking them when they were sick. Some favorite books shared were *James and the Giant Peach, The Secret Garden*, and *Anne of Green Gables*. When the children became older she enjoyed laughing with them and their teenage friends. She would even cry with them when disappointments came their way.

Pat was a conscientious mother in every respect—encouraging and helping her children with their schoolwork, extracurricular activities, and talents, and in developing healthy eating habits. She served them nutritious meals and abstained from the "fast food" trend of the day. But Mary Alice does remember one humorous exception to this practice which might be of solace to those who have sometimes "cut corners." One time Pat was planning to travel with her husband, Jeff, on a church assignment. The children would be left to care for themselves. So that they would not be burdened with the preparation of meals, she decided that for this short period she would purchase some precooked meals which they could warm up quickly.

However, she did not want anyone (particularly BYU students) to presume that this was her regular practice. She donned some large sunglasses, covered her dress with a long coat, and in this disguise quickly went to Albertsons to buy some frozen pizzas, Hungry Man TV dinners, and frozen chicken pot pies. For the duration of this trip the children dined on those "quickie meals" with enjoyment. But as soon as Pat returned, they again were fed her own cooking, with plenty of dark green and yellow vegetables, generous amounts of fresh fruit, and the lighter meats including chicken and fish. Did anyone detect Pat in her disguise at Albertsons? No one knows, but she certainly hoped not!

Although Pat would state that her greatest desire has been to love her children and rear them in righteousness, anyone who knows her recognizes that her influence has stretched far beyond her family. When she and her husband and children were living in the President's Home on campus, Pat invited a nephew from St. George to live with them for a six-month period. Another time she invited a young Vietnamese student to live with them and helped him adjust to the United States and prepare to attend BYU.

When she was working in the General Young Women presidency, thousands of students heard her bear her testimony of the principles of the Church. With her husband she co-authored two books, published by Deseret Book, titled *However Long and Hard the Road*, and *On Earth as it is in Heaven*. These books contain the beliefs and thoughts of this remarkable husband and wife team, both of whom have dedicated themselves to all the principles of The Church of Jesus Christ of Latter-day Saints.

Jeffrey Holland resigned from his position as president of BYU when he was called to the First Quorum of Seventy. Later he was called to the Council of the Twelve Apostles, an event that led to an article featuring the Hollands in the *Brigham Young Magazine*. The following are excerpts:

"Both my call to the First Quorum of Seventy in 1989 and now to the apostleship have involved real soul searching and genuine spiritual examination," says Elder Holland. "But this call, in particular, has caused me deep physical and spiritual anguish. I know, intellectually, what has happened, but from an emotional and spiritual standpoint, accepting the reality is going to take a very long time.

"Since this call came, I have gone many nights without sleep. The magnitude of this responsibility has just been consuming."

Sister Holland, likewise, has shared in the feelings her husband has had since being called and ordained on June 23, 1994. . . .

"I remember as a young wife," she recalls, "how deeply in love I was with my husband and how I once said to my mother, 'I don't know what I would do if Jeff ever had a calling in the ward that took him away from home for any length of time.' But I quickly came to see the great love he has for people, and I've experienced the joy that has come through his—and, in a small measure, our—service to others." . . .

To this Sister Holland adds, "There have been a lot of humbling experiences that we have lived through, and while I don't know that the Lord pushes them into our lives, I do believe he allows them to happen. What we learned so many times at BYU—and at other times in our life—is that He is our only source of strength." . . .

And so the Hollands struggle—both with accepting and adjusting to an overwhelming new calling, and with finally settling into their home five years after having moved from BYU.[3]

These two united individuals certainly approached Elder Holland's calling with sincere humility. And although the

Hollands recognize that the Lord is their source of strength, it is clear that Elder Holland has always drawn much from Patricia's encouragement and spirit. The Holland children recall that their mother's spirituality has always been one of her greatest strengths. Their earliest memories include seeing their mother kneel by the side of her bed pouring her soul out to the Lord. Likewise, it is hard for them to recall a day in which they didn't find their mother spending some time pondering and studying the scriptures. She has always carried a set in her purse in case she has to wait in a line or is caught in a traffic jam. One of her favorite scriptures pertains to all of us: "Trust in the Lord with all thine heart, and lean not to thine own understanding" (Proverbs 3:5).

Patricia has touched many lives through quiet example. For example, her husband recalls walking into the bedroom one day after school to find both Pat and two-year-old Mary curled up on the bed reading their scriptures. While Pat read and highlighted her scriptures with a red pencil, Mary followed suit with her small set of scriptures and a red crayon.

Patricia Terry Holland will continue to gently influence the lives of her children, grandchildren, and others throughout the world. But her influence will, as it has been in the past, be felt primarily by her husband who loves her wholly and reveres her as his example and strength in living the teachings of the Savior Jesus Christ.

Janet Griffin Lee

by

Diana Lee Allred, assisted by Jan Nelson Ekeroth

Janet Lee's life has been an example of remarkable and unselfish service to others. With President Rex E. Lee's recent death, their book, Marathon of Faith (Deseret Book, 1996), has been published. In this book, Janet and Rex provide a moving account of their life together— from their courtship up through Rex Lee's struggle with cancer and his tenure as BYU president. Some of the following details about the Lees' early courtship are taken from this book. The remainder of the sketch is a personal tribute to Janet Lee by her oldest daughter, Diana Lee Allred.

*W*hen Janet Griffin and a boyfriend were visiting Janet's parents in Mexico City, somehow they ended up in a car driven by a young missionary, Elder Rex E. Lee, who was serving as a counselor in the Mexican mission presidency (the Griffins were friends of the mission president). Janet was completely oblivious to the elder driving the car, but he, undaunted by the boyfriend sitting beside her, adjusted his rearview mirror to keep an eye on her.

On another visit, after Janet's parents had repeatedly tried to interest her in this elder, Janet became annoyed, declaring, "I have heard enough about this 'paragon of virtue,' and I am going to make a public statement. I am not interested in Rex Lee; I will never be interested in Rex Lee; in fact, I don't even know Rex Lee. But I don't think I like him at all." [1]

But after Janet had had more time to observe Elder Lee, and her parents had persisted in mentioning him in their calls and letters, her dislike for him seemed to soften—though she still wasn't sure what to think of him. Then when Rex and Janet bumped into each other on his first day back at BYU after his mission (the spring of 1958), and he subsequently asked her out, Janet begrudgingly allowed him to take her to church with him on Sunday (she already had dates for Friday and Saturday).

Their first encounters were rocky. Rex tried to convince Janet that both her boyfriend and her major were wrong for her. And then, when he followed their date up with a phone call that Janet found irritating, she returned to her original opinion of him. Her daughter, Diana, tells of the experience and the final outcome:

It seems that Dad called Mom the next morning and, with a partner, sang the following humorous song:

> I tried so hard, my dear, to show
> That you're my every dream,
> Yet every time I see your face
> It makes me want to scream.

You look much better to me, dear,
The further we're apart.
Your liver may be warm
But you've got a cold, cold heart.

Singing a song was Dad's way of telling a girl he liked her. He would then hang up immediately. So, instead of getting an explanation for such bizarre behavior, Mom got a click of the telephone. No explanation. No response. Just a song. "Cold, cold heart indeed," she thought. Knowing instinctively who had called her, Mom told her roommate that she would never go out with that strange fellow again. Dad, on the other hand, thought he had given his date the supreme compliment by singing to her. The words of the song he had sung were irrelevant. The important thing was that he had serenaded her.

Obviously, his approach worked. I don't know if it was my father's persistence or my mother's indulgence, but they were engaged by the following November and married the next July.

Continuing in Diana Lee Allred's words, we now learn from a personal perspective about Janet Lee's life of love and service—for her husband, children, and Brigham Young University.

My mother, Janet Griffin Lee, was born to Ben and Marian Griffin on October 22, 1939, in Paris, France; she is the middle child of three. My grandfather, who worked as an attaché for the U.S. Treasury Department, was transferred regularly, and as a result, my mother lived in several different states and many countries, including France, Mexico, and Japan. In fact, she never lived in the same area longer than three years. This lifestyle has probably contributed the most to her incredible resiliency and adaptability. She has needed both, given my father's varied career.

Mother's love of children prompted her to enroll in the elementary education program at Brigham Young University, where she earned her bachelor's degree in 1960. Periodically during her married life, Mom used her degree to teach, first in Chicago while my dad was in law school, and years later at a private school in McLean, Virginia, where she developed a phonics curriculum that was adopted and used by many public schools in northern Virginia.

She is the mother of seven—Diana, Tom, Wendy, Michael, Stephanie, Melissa, and Christie—and a grandmother to twelve. She always considers her family top priority and has given each of us a strong sense of security, a belief in our own worth, and a desire to succeed. She is patient, loving, and always open-minded.

All my life, I have watched in awe as my talented mother has not only accepted life's challenges but has made each experience a positive one. Perhaps the best example of this attitude was the way she handled my father's cancer. From the beginning, she assured all of us that everything would be okay, that we would survive whatever hardship we were asked to bear. Even in the most difficult moments—from verification of my father's first cancer in 1987, to the devastating confirmation of the second incurable form three years later—her faith was strong and her testimony unwavering. Around the house, she made sure the family members talked positively with one another. There were too many other exciting and important subjects to talk about to dwell on depressing thoughts of an illness that was still so unknown. Of course, the greatest benefactor of her positive attitude was my father. She was loving and encouraging toward him every step of the way—in the moments of joy as well as the moments of great pain.

When my father was first diagnosed with cancer, he was treated at the National Institute of Health in Bethesda, Maryland. During this hospitalization my mother remained at his bedside during the entire ordeal. Through it all, he became more keenly aware of her complete loyalty and support. I believe he was able to live as long as he did and serve as president of BYU because of her. And when he died recently, Mom had prepared herself and the family so well, that his passing was peaceful and beautiful. We were all present when he died.

During my childhood, my mother was just, but fair. Before a punishment was ever given, she allowed us to express our feelings and plead our cause. She would listen intently, judge fairly, and act accordingly. I never felt I was punished unjustly. In fact, she used to tell me that I taught her too—that sometimes I was right and she was wrong.

On one such occasion, when I was eight years old, I had been asked to care for Michael, my one-year-old brother who was taking a nap, while Mom went to the grocery store. I wanted to help, but I also wanted to play with a neighboring girlfriend. Unwisely I chose to go play, leaving Michael with my six-year-old sister, Wendy. When Mom returned she was upset—upset that I had been disobedient and had used such bad judgment. She immediately meted out what seemed to me a death sentence. I was to be "grounded" for an entire week. Completely grounded! But true to her sense of fairness, she was still open to negotiation. After I presented my feelings, we were able to work out a compromise. I would be grounded, but only for two days. And for the rest of the week, I would not be allowed certain privileges. To me, this arrangement seemed more realistic, and I appreciated my mother's willingness to listen and negotiate. This was the only time in my life that Mom used this disciplinary method, and since I was such a social young lady, I was grateful for that. Best of all, though, I was grateful that my mother was never too proud to say "I'm sorry," especially to her children. That made us feel important and worthwhile.

My mother has a close relationship with each of her children. When I was young, she regularly sat on my bed and listened to me as long as I needed her. I remember one particularly difficult time when we moved from Provo to Washington, D.C., so my dad could assume the position of assistant attorney general for the United States. Leaving my friends behind in Provo was almost more than I could bear. I was small for my age, I didn't have a single friend in my new school, and I was sure nothing in my world would seem right again. At the time, Mom was expecting my sister, Melissa, but she still wanted to spend hours at my bedside, comforting me, encouraging me, and telling me just the right words to lift my spirits. She would tell me what a good daughter I was, how smart and beautiful I was, and how much she loved me. I have no doubt that my healthy self-esteem comes from her.

The remarkable thing about this experience, and many others like it, is that Mom showed the same deep concern for all seven of her children and her husband. Her time was our time, and each of us has felt Mom's total support. One of her finest gifts is her ability to help others feel happy, even in their darkest hours. Our family has certainly benefited from that gift, and so have countless others.

Although Mom has had an extremely busy life as a wife and mother, she has always done her share in the Church as well. She has worked in all the auxiliaries—Primary, Sunday School, Young Women, and Relief Society. Perhaps her favorite calling has been with the Young Women, where she has been the Laurel advisor and Young Women president for a number of years. Since she has five daughters, the Young Women organization seems to suit her. And she suits it—she works well with the girls this age. With her own teenage daughters and sons, Mom has been loving, yet firm, reminding them that they must be home from dates by a certain hour. She would always wait up for us to be sure we came in by the agreed-upon time.

As I grew older, Mom's life became more complicated and demanding, but she continued to stay very involved in my life, even when I married and had children of my own. When I was a teenager, she used to wake up at 6:30 *every* morning to jog with me for an hour. Those times we spent together are priceless to me now. I didn't realize then what sacrifices she was making for me, especially since she had six younger children at home. It was nearly the only time we had to be alone together and our conversations ranged from schoolwork, to dating, to cheerleading, to gospel and moral ideals. Even today, with all but one child married, she still jogs with her daughters early in the morning. We jog at a nice steady pace so we can talk, but still complete a daily six-mile distance. On Saturdays, when our schedules are not so stressful, we sometimes jog as many as ten miles. Not long ago, Mom and three of her daughters competed in the St. George, Utah, Marathon. Quite a feat for a woman in her fifties!

During my dad's time as BYU president, Mom spent about one-third of her time as an unpaid but very valuable member of the BYU administrative team. Though she never sought the position, being BYU's "first lady" was a natural role for her. She is a gracious hostess with an ability to make everyone feel welcome, comfortable, and accepted. One of her favorite activities was hosting lunches for women faculty members and faculty wives in her home. She has enjoyed the friendships she has made with so many marvelous BYU women, whose talents and skills are so varied, abundant, and interesting.

My mother has a gift for writing and delivering talks—a gift I watched her cultivate during my dad's tenure as BYU president. An animated speaker, she would address not only the students and faculty twice a year at BYU's devotional assemblies, but also countless smaller groups on and off campus. She rarely refused an invitation. Her joint talks with my father are frequently rebroadcast in the early mornings on KBYU–Channel 11.

Mom's talks usually include illustrations from her personal or family life. Her pink crayon talk tells of her daughter, Stephanie, who, when told on her first day of school to pick her favorite color of crayon to write her name, refused to act, even though she was perfectly capable of writing her name. When asked later why she wouldn't do what she was told, Stephanie explained that she couldn't write her name because her favorite color—pink—was not in the box. Mom drew a parallel from this: when life does not give us exactly what we think we want or need, we should never stand still, as Stephanie had done. Rather we must adapt to our circumstances and keep progressing. Mom has received a number of letters from students thanking her for such pieces of advice and wisdom from her talks.

One of the things I've always admired most about my mother is her intelligence. She is a voracious reader—of Church material, the daily newspaper, and, before my dad died, the latest cancer research. In fact, Mom read so much about Dad's two types of cancer that his doctors came to respect her insights and advice. She even kept the doctors straight on all the drugs he was taking, and their compatibility. Among family and friends, Mom became known as Dr. Lee—a title well earned, considering that Dad survived as the longest living patient with his particular combination of two cancers.

For eighteen years I had a mother who nurtured and loved me, who taught me right from wrong, and who instilled in me a strong testimony and a sense of worth. And then something wonderful happened: we became best friends. She let me grow up and now respects me as an adult. We give each other advice and laugh and cry together as best friends do. It is the most rich and rewarding relationship I could ever hope to have with my mother. And I am quite sure that all six other children in the family would say the same of her. If I could come close to doing for my husband and children what she has done for me and my family, I feel I will have achieved my purpose in life.

Marilyn Scholes Bateman

by

Michael J. Bateman

Faithful, committed, and fun-loving, Marilyn Bateman has had just the right qualities to help her through many moves and intense periods of professional and Church service with her husband, BYU President Merrill J. Bateman. Marilyn has raised seven children and now has twenty grandchildren. She currently serves the BYU community in her role as "first lady."

*T*he greatest inheritance of man is a posterity. The greatest inheritance of a posterity is a Christian ancestry." These words, written by Frederick Scholes, paternal grandfather of Marilyn Scholes Bateman, embody what is most important to Marilyn Bateman—family and the gospel of Jesus Christ.

Marilyn Scholes was born September 29, 1937, in Logan, Utah. At the time, her father, Harold Burnham Scholes, was a forestry student at the Utah State Agricultural College. During his college years, he worked for the U.S. Forest Service to support his family. Those were the Depression years, so times were difficult; nobody had much of anything. The Scholes family was no exception. On the day of Marilyn's birth, her father was on assignment with the Forest Service in a nearby canyon and could not be reached. Her mother, Orale Wayman Scholes, was surprised that the new baby was arriving early. She made arrangements for the care of her oldest child, called a taxi, and went alone to the hospital, where she immediately gave birth to a baby daughter. Marilyn Scholes was the couple's first daughter and second child.

Marilyn never knew her maternal grandparents, who had died when her mother was a small girl. However, she was greatly influenced by her paternal grandparents, Frederick and Lydia Abalona Burnham Scholes. In a newsletter for a Scholes family reunion, Marilyn wrote, "This experience of writing and editing the family newsletter has renewed in me the great pride I have in being a Scholes. I always knew we were an exceptional bunch. We were all truly born of goodly parents and grandparents. Our heritage is rich." Pride in her name and love for her family and church were instilled in Marilyn by her progenitors, and she, in turn, has passed these values on to her children and grandchildren.

In the Scholes family, Marilyn's grandparents also cultivated a love and respect for temples and for the beauty of God's creations. Her Grandfather Scholes served as temple recorder in the Logan temple for more than forty years. Often the grandchildren would hike "Temple Hill" to meet Grandpa Scholes after work and walk with him the half mile to his home. One of Frederick Scholes's hobbies was writing down unusual names and name combinations that he came across while recording names in the temple, such as Doolittle Brainhead, Sara Gotobed, White Lamb, Abel Seaman, Orange Peel, and Ima Darling.

Frederick Scholes and his parents were English immigrants, and throughout his life, Fred retained his pride in his English heritage. One manifestation was his love of flowers. Fred was famous for his "wildflower" garden, which covered approximately one acre of land behind the home. He spent many hours with his children and grand-children in the garden, teaching lessons about nature and God's cre-ations. One of his sons expressed his appreciation for the garden: "From Dad I learned to feel a partnership with the Creator in growing plants, especially in hybridizing and developing new creations. Dad often said that gardening was good for the soul and that you never heard of a flower and plant lover being guilty of a serious crime." This garden also provided income for the children's educations: the fami-ly cut and sold flowers for Memorial Day and other events.

When World War II broke out, Marilyn's family moved from Logan to Salt Lake City, where her father went to work as a quality control supervisor for the Remington Arms munitions factory. After the war, the family then moved to American Fork where she spent the rest of her childhood and youth.

The Scholes children learned to work hard and be responsible—they shared the housework and chores and earned their own money for clothes and personal needs. As a girl of ten or twelve, Marilyn earned extra money by babysitting and doing housework for neigh-bors. As a teenager and young adult, she always had a job, whether at Don's Sweetshop—the local hamburger hangout—or later as a mes-senger girl in the rolling plant at Geneva Steel.

Marilyn jokes that her family could easily have originated family home evening, because they always loved to be together, playing board games, camping, hiking, having water fights in the backyard, and going to brothers' ball games. Marilyn inherited many of her father's fun-loving and adventurous characteristics. When she was thirteen, she and her best friend had an adventure that has become one of the most notorious stories of her youth. The two girls borrowed an aunt's old pickup truck and drove from American Fork to Salt Lake City and back (sixty miles round trip), one steering and the other shifting gears. But family and friends who had been searching for the missing girls caught them red-handed when they returned.

It was this fun-loving personality that appealed to a young man attending Marilyn's high school. Merrill Bateman was a year older than Marilyn, a serious student, and perhaps less adventurous and outgoing. But sometimes opposites attract. The two began to date in their late high-school and early college years. After Merrill graduated from American Fork High School in 1954, he enrolled at the University of Utah where he completed two years of college before serving a mission for The Church of Jesus Christ of Latter-day Saints in the British Isles.

Following Marilyn's graduation from high school, she entered Brigham Young University. In addition to her studies, Marilyn participated in extracurricular activities, including the Cougarettes. After one year at BYU, Marilyn spent six months working for a savings and loan company in southern California in order to earn enough money for additional study. She then returned to Utah and attended a year of school at the LDS Business College. Marilyn and Merrill wrote to each other during his mission years, and soon after Merrill returned home, they became engaged.

The Batemans were married in the Salt Lake Temple on March 23, 1959. They made Salt Lake City their first home, since Merrill had slightly more than a year left on his bachelor's degree in economics at the University of Utah. During the 1959–60 school year, Merrill completed his undergraduate work, and Marilyn also attended the university. Education has always been a high priority in the Bateman home, and Marilyn and Merrill have expected good grades and citizenship from the children. Marilyn, too, has continued her education, even after having five of her seven children. In 1968, she returned to BYU to complete another year of college. Over the years she has accumulated more than 120 hours of university credit in between many moves and seven children.

Michael, the Batemans' first child, was born on April 14, 1960. The following summer, the family left Utah for the east coast where

Merrill entered a Ph.D. program at the Massachusetts Institute of Technology. This was the beginning of many opportunities, challenges, and adventures for the Bateman family. Marilyn says of that time: "Those days were the refiner's fire for us. This was the first time in my life I had been away from home. My husband and I were just learning to be parents. For Merrill it was a difficult period because this was the first time in his career as a student that he had been truly challenged—he was feeling the pressure. And on top of all this, we were living on a shoestring."

Their second child, Mark, was born on March 26, 1962, while Marilyn and Merrill were living in Boston. Later that year a life-changing opportunity presented itself. Merrill was invited to serve as a lecturer at the University of Ghana in West Africa, where he would also gather data for his doctoral thesis. At the time, Ghana was under martial law. On the day Marilyn and Merrill arrived, there was an assassination attempt on Kwame Nkrumah, the Ghanaian leader. Fear of a coup filled the air and security was extremely tight. Everywhere they went they saw guards with machetes or guns. The culture shock of living in an underdeveloped country filled with political upheaval was enormous for Marilyn, a young wife and mother who was lonely, a world away from home, and concerned for the safety of her two small sons.

Within a few weeks of their arrival, Marilyn learned that she was expecting another child. Two weeks after that, Mark, their nine-month-old son, developed a high fever. The baby had contracted malaria despite his parents' efforts to feed him anti-malaria pills. Although he responded to medication, Mark then came down with dengue fever (jungle fever) as soon as the malaria medicine had started to take effect. The new illness was even more severe than the malaria had been and caused excruciating headaches and even higher temperatures. The stress of the baby's illness, the lack of proper medical facilities, a new pregnancy, and the difficulty of being in foreign surroundings combined to make the situation intolerable for Marilyn.

She writes, "I told my husband I couldn't stay there any longer. I felt the hardships were too much to bear. Merrill understood. He replied that even if I had to leave he could not. He had made a commitment and had to stay until it was completed. I returned home alone with the two little boys."

Back in Utah, Marilyn realized something that changed the course of her own and her family's lives. Even though she was back in more comfortable circumstances, she felt a sense of failure. She describes this period of time: "I wasn't really happy when I got home. I felt I had failed my husband. I knew I had been unable to cope with the challenge that we had both accepted. It wasn't just his challenge; it was my challenge as well—to be by his side, to support and encourage him. It wasn't that he felt I had failed, or that I was no longer there with him. It was that I had failed to live up to the expectations I had for myself. Until we were together again, I experienced only difficulty and disappointment in my life. In a way, I suppose it may have been a blessing in disguise, because it was a turning point. It was a time of expanding commitment to my family." This defining period became a foundation of strength for Marilyn and Merrill during the next thirty-plus years of marriage and family life.

Marilyn has been challenged in many ways since those early days in Africa, but her increased commitment created a stable home life through the Bateman's nineteen moves during their first twenty years of marriage. "Mom" is the glue that has kept the family together. Because of Merrill's career and church responsibilities, the primary responsibility for raising the children has been hers. As in her family growing up, family activities are important to Marilyn as a mother. Music lessons, ball games, trips to Lake Powell, family night, and vacations have all been integral to the Bateman way of life.

Marilyn and Merrill have seven children and twenty grandchildren. Always a keeper of traditions, Marilyn makes each birthday special. For example, she always hung poster-sized pictures of the birthday child on the kitchen walls when the children were young. Now even the grandchildren have certain expectations about holidays because of the family traditions their grandparents have maintained. Other important family traditions include father's blessings, missions, and temple marriages. All four sons and one daughter served missions, and each missionary knew they could count on a weekly letter from their mother. Six of the children are now married, each in the temple.

Marilyn has been an excellent role model for her three daughters. Michele, her oldest, says of her mother, "I grew up wanting to be a wife and mother because of Mom's example. She was always available for us. Whenever I did have difficulty locating her, I could usually find her doing one of two things—reading a book or praying." Merilee, another daughter, says, "I knew my mother was totally committed to the gospel. She made sure we had family prayer each day." Melisa says, "She has taught me the importance of fasting and praying with a purpose."

Like her husband, Marilyn has served in many capacities within the Church. She served in both stake and ward Relief Society presidencies, as a stake missionary, as a visiting teacher, and as a Relief Society teacher. One of her most challenging yet rewarding callings was as the Spiritual Living teacher in Relief Society. She worked for hours to prepare each lesson. Her greatest desire was to provide a message and environment that would spiritually lift each sister in the ward.

One of Marilyn's unique qualities is her sensitivity toward others. She has often befriended the friendless and accepted people into her home for extended periods of time. As she has traveled around the world with her husband—particularly in recent years on Church assignments—she has become friends with many Latter-day Saint women.

Her sensitivity to other people's feelings has had its poignant moments. In 1971, the Bateman family moved to England, where Merrill accepted employment with Mars Ltd. At the time, their youngest children were four-year-old twin daughters, Merilee and Melisa. The Batemans decided that the girls would attend the village school, so Marilyn drove the girls to the schoolhouse on the first day. Before she could get the girls out of the car, however, they locked all the doors. Like many young children, they were apprehensive about attending school for the first time. For several minutes both Marilyn and the teacher tried to coax the crying girls into opening the car. Marilyn grew more worried by the minute, until finally the girls opened the doors. Reluctantly, Marilyn led them inside the school and left them—still crying—with the teacher. The teacher was not so tenderhearted. When the girls continued to cry after Marilyn left, the teacher promptly marched them to a nearby closet where she locked them in for the better part of the day. Marilyn didn't learn about the closet episode until years later.

The past four years have brought significant changes to the Bateman family. In 1992, Merrill was called to serve as a member of the Second Quorum of Seventy for the Church. A year later he was assigned to the Asia North Area presidency, where he supervised the work of the Church in Japan and Korea. Serving together as representatives of the Church was a marvelous experience for Marilyn and Merrill. Their letters home were filled with spiritual experiences. Many times Merrill wrote of how the Saints—particularly the Japanese and Korean sisters—were drawn to Marilyn. He would often mention her way of making people feel comfortable and included. But their stay in Asia was cut short—it lasted only nine months. Since they had developed such a great love for the people in that area, it was difficult for them to leave. But a new call had come. In the April 1994 Saturday morning session of General Conference, Merrill Bateman was called as the Presiding Bishop of the Church. Merrill and Marilyn had learned of the change a few days before, but the rest of the family found out as they listened to General Conference. Within a few short weeks, the Batemans returned to Utah.

Perhaps their frequent moving during the first twenty years of marriage prepared Marilyn and Merrill for such short and intense opportunities. The call as Presiding Bishop was also brief. In January 1996, Merrill was called to be the eleventh president of Brigham Young University and a member of the First Quorum of Seventy.

With each change, Marilyn has remained by her husband's side. It hasn't always been easy. She has a quote she refers to in challenging times: "Life is what happens to you when you have other things planned." Marilyn was prepared at an early age to value family, church, and God's creations. And her defining moment occurred almost thirty-five years ago following her return from Africa. Since then, her commitment to marriage, family, and the gospel has shaped the lives of her children and grandchildren and touched the lives of many other people worldwide.

Cheryl Brown

Associate Academic Vice-President

by

CindaLee Hall

Cheryl Brown's faith, kindness, and dedication, along with her outstanding teaching and academic records, make her the kind of leader and scholar at BYU that many students and colleagues admire. Her recent appointment as Associate Academic Vice-President over International, Distance, and Continuing Education follows many years of sustained service and achievement.

*C*heryl Brown is from a large and very close family. "I grew up in Cedar City, Utah, and am the youngest of ten children," she says. "My oldest brother is old enough to be my father. When I was little, one day I said to my mother, 'How come we have such a big family?' Someone piped up and said, 'Well, if we didn't have such a big family we wouldn't have you.' Scott, my brother who's down the line too said, 'Nor me neither!' I sat there and thought and thought. Finally I said, 'Scott and I would have just come walking down the road.'"

Cheryl feels it is fun being in a large family and says, "being the last one, I have a better sense of the whole family than anybody else because I was the only one that grew up with the whole family intact. I think that happens to a lot of youngest children."

Born June 19, 1945, to Althea Lund and John Middleton Brown, Cheryl took important steps early. She tells the story of one early decision that shaped her attitudes for life. "When I was somewhere between eight and ten, the circumstances were such that everybody was always feeling sorry for themselves. I was able to see that it didn't have a positive effect on other people and I remember vowing, 'I will never feel sorry for myself.' It was wonderful; it has carried me through all kinds of things because everybody has things happen that are not the way we want them to go. That resolution to never feel sorry for myself has made a real difference in my life."

Education has always been important to Cheryl. Her father gave up his schooling and dream of being a doctor or lawyer soon after high school because he needed to help his widowed mother run her farm. As a result, he always stressed the importance of higher education with his children. Even though he never realized his dreams, all his children have college educations and six of the ten have doctoral degrees.

Cheryl's original dream was to be a medical doctor, influenced by four members of her family—two of her brothers are doctors, one is a dentist, and one a veterinarian. Her early decision to be a doctor changed, however, after a conversation with a brother who was studying medicine at the time. He asked her, "If you get married, do you intend to keep practicing?" Her answer was, "No, I want to stay home with the family." Then he said, "Well, there are only a limited number of seats in medical school. If you take one of the seats and then don't practice medicine, what you've done essentially is robbed the world of a doctor." She thought about it and decided what she really wanted to do was have a family and raise children.

That Cheryl has not married nor had the children she desired has been difficult for her, but her attitude about it, as with everything else, is positive. Cheryl feels she has a happy life. She has wonderful friends and her large family; she tries to hold close to her family and do things that will help keep them together. Cheryl says of her life, "You don't intend to be single. My greatest desire was to get married and have twelve children, but it just didn't ever come about that way. I've had opportunities to marry, but they weren't right. Sometimes I prayed about it and knew it wasn't right, and sometimes we prayed about it together and knew it.

"But as far as what to do if you don't marry, my experience has been that the Lord will give you 'next steps.' I love the old saying, 'The Lord can't guide your footsteps if you won't move your feet.' You have to keep moving, and if you are trying to do what's right, if you're living the gospel, he can guide your footsteps to where he can use you—where it will be of most good for you and the people around you. He's given me opportunities I never dreamed of because the dreams I had in other areas weren't the ways he wanted me to go."

Cheryl's decision not to become a doctor meant changing plans for her entire future. She had decided to go to BYU after high school, but in praying about the decision could find no peace. She finally decided to go to Utah State University and felt this was where the Lord wanted her to be. She says, "This is probably not the best thing to tell BYU people, but I did what Doctrine and Covenants, section 9 says: study it out in your mind. I was drawn to BYU because of the Church, and I felt strongly for the Church things. So I studied it out in my mind and decided to go to BYU. But the decision wouldn't ever settle—I never felt peace. And then one night my best friend at Utah State called and said, 'Hey, you've just got to come here.' I said O.K. just that quickly and felt immediate peace—total peace. I went to Utah State and had a great experience."

After graduating from USU with a B.A. in American Studies, Cheryl was called in 1968 to serve a mission in Chile. There Cheryl, for whom it is so important not to complain or indulge in self-pity, learned a lesson in humility from a bout of hepatitis. She says, "I can remember growing up wanting to go on a mission. But I'd heard all kinds of stories about lady missionaries who were always sick. So I vowed, 'I am never going to be that way. I am going to be the best possible lady missionary there is.' I went out, worked hard, and got hepatitis, but I ignored it because I wasn't going to be sick. I went for days and it got worse and worse. After a while, I couldn't eat, and finally, one day, I couldn't get off the bed—I was that sick. What I learned is that you don't even take a breath without the Lord willing it—only through his grace could I be any kind of missionary at all. After that, I wanted to be a good missionary, not out of a selfish desire to be the best possible missionary, but because I was grateful for the opportunity from the Lord."

Following her mission, Cheryl returned to Utah State University where she earned an M.A. in English. Her ability to speak Spanish fluently (from her mission) put her in a position to teach ESL (English as a Second Language) at USU and later at BYU, where she earned another M.A., this time in TESL (Teaching English as a Second Language). Her Ph.D., which she earned in 1983 from UCLA, is in applied linguistics.

Since joining the BYU faculty in 1975, Cheryl has researched, presented, and published extensively in the field of language acquisition, especially on the ways second-language learners acquire the subtle and complex connotations of language—inferences a learner can pick up beyond the obvious meanings of words. She has also been a leader in numerous professional organizations in her field. Not only is Cheryl an impressive teacher herself—she has won a number of outstanding teaching awards, including the Karl G. Maeser Distinguished Teaching Award in 1986—but she has also been instrumental in training many other teachers of language.

In addition to her teaching for the BYU Linguistics Department, Cheryl has taught Book of Mormon classes (which she admits are her favorite classes to teach) and given addresses and presentations at university devotionals, BYU Women's Conferences, and the annual Book of Mormon Symposiums at BYU. She has also served as Associate Dean of the College of Humanities. Some of Cheryl's finest opportunities have come through a Fulbright professorship at the

University of Arica in Chile. There she has been able to share the latest developments in language acquisition and be back among the people she served on her mission. She delights in the progress the Church has made in Chile.

Teaching is one of Cheryl's greatest joys in life. She always gets excited when one of her students finally finishes a thesis or takes other important steps in life. Her colleagues confirm this love and admire Cheryl's willingness to really get involved with her students. Belva Burgess, the Linguistics Department secretary, says that graduate students always ask for her as their thesis chair because they know how much she cares.

Recently Cheryl was appointed Associate Academic Vice-President over International, Distance, and Continuing Education. An associate dean of the College of Humanities, Edward Geary, who also shared that position with Cheryl before she was appointed vice-president, says, "I think one of the most revealing things about her is that she refuses to get the O sticker that lets you park in the special reserved parking. She continues to park in the faculty parking lot. I tease her that she's in denial. She's refusing to accept the idea that she's an administrator by insisting on being an ordinary faculty member. Obviously what she cares about most is teaching and her students. The assignment she has now is frustrating for her because she can only teach one class a year. So it's like being taken away from her life, yet she has, at the same time, exactly the understanding of education needed for the assignment there. It's a kind of paradox—all her life she has prepared herself to be a good teacher, yet in furthering the educational process for BYU, she's been taken out of the classroom and put into meetings."

When asked about her current position as a vice-president for BYU, Cheryl's reply is, "The one thing I like about it is that it's a place where I can work with and influence a lot of people. The potential is there to bless many."

Although Cheryl no longer has the opportunity to teach as frequently, she continues to use her many talents to bless the lives of those around her—in fact, all who are associated with BYU. Her work ethic encourages others and her charitable spirit reaches many as she strives to "move her feet" while the Lord guides her footsteps.

Lillian Clayson Booth (Davis)

Counselor of Women

by

Wayne Clayson Booth and Lucille Booth Bushnell

Lillian Clayson Booth (Davis) served as BYU's Counselor of Women from 1945 to 1959. Her enormous dedication and her great capacity for sensitive listening and wise counsel made her a valued advisor in her family, the Church, the community, and in her work at BYU. Students, family members, and friends benefitted from her wisdom and love.

*N*o one who had witnessed from the outside the constricted circumstances of Lillian Clayson's childhood could have believed that she would one day become one of the most widely beloved and influential of Brigham Young University's teachers and administrators. She was born November 30, 1894, in the tiny village of Lake Shore, Utah. Her parents had been impoverished children of working-class converts who had come from England to Utah in the 1860s. Her father, Eli J. Clayson, had lost his father when he was ten; his mother, Lillian's grandmother, became a shoemaker's assistant, and Eli, working to help support his younger brothers and sisters, had to postpone most of his education until his twenties. By the time of her birth, they were barely able to make ends meet. Lillian's mother, Ann Elizabeth Hawkins, was born to parents who had even fewer educational opportunities.

Indeed, the tasks of simple economic survival are more prominent in her memories of childhood than educational aspirations. As she wrote in her brief autobiography:

> I thought there could not be a place on this earth where there was so much work. There were as many as seven hundred quarts of fruits, vegetables, and juices bottled each year. Meat was salted down also. Most of the fruit was grown and picked from our own place. I can still see mother and all of us children up early in the morning with our pails going out to pick raspberries and Old English currants. I'm fond of raspberries and currants, but to this day, if I had to pick them, I'd prefer not to have them.

But anyone who could have looked inside and discovered her grandparents' and parents' true ideals would not now be quite so surprised to learn from scores of former students that her warm wisdom and compassionate caring exercised a crucial influence on their lives. Her family believed passionately in the importance of obtaining an education, not simply as a way of getting ahead but also as obedience to a divine command. They believed, and often quoted to her and to us, her children, what the gospel taught: man cannot be saved in ignorance.

Her father pursued that belief, and some years before she was born, he chose to suffer the humiliation of returning to high school at the age of twenty-one, ill-clothed and often hungry, to study alongside scoffing teenagers. He then attended college and became a teacher. Though her mother had to leave school after the eighth grade, she had become a reader, managing somehow to find time, through all those domestic chores that Lillian remembered as oppressive, to read many of the works of poetry, fiction, and history that the family had steadily accumulated. She read aloud, first to Lillian, and then to each of the other seven children. One child, Wayne, remembers how wonderful it was, at age seven, to have his grandmother read stories to him. Lillian thus quickly learned that, along with other duties, getting an education ranked very high. Nobody was surprised when she became the valedictorian at the 1914 American Fork High School graduation.

Those burdensome domestic economies—symbolized by Lillian's repeated memory of the "seven hundred annual bottlings"— were devoted to not just survival but to a higher purpose as well: every child should receive as much formal education and mission experience as could be afforded. All of the Clayson's eight children attended BYU and most of them graduated. Most of them served as missionaries, and Lillian, being the eldest, worked to help the others attain these goals. All of them had music lessons. Lillian became an accomplished pianist and in high school supplemented the family money by playing for a dance band and teaching piano. Piano and organ became a permanent part of her life. She played both instruments for all the different wards and stakes she attended, and at age fifty settled down to conscientious organ study. She became so proficient in her organ playing that she accompanied many stake conferences in the Provo Tabernacle.

On her maximum salary of one hundred dollars a month, it was never easy. In 1915, Lillian had to stop college after one year and a "normal certificate" to help support her younger brothers and sister, and then, after her marriage, to support her husband in getting his degree. She later wrote:

> If I were taking my university work now, I would never think of not going four years while I was at it. But when I was a girl, I felt that if I got one year and taught I was lucky. I felt that was all my people could afford to send me since seven others had to get col-

lege work. So my aim was a Normal Diploma. I thought I did
well to get that.

She devoted herself to what she hoped would be a large family. A
June bride, she married Wayne Chipman Booth, the valedictorian of
a previous high school class, in 1919. At that time she surely would
have been astonished at the interpretation we can now give to the
patriarchal blessing she received after a year or two of teaching.

> Thou art required to prepare thyself to wield a mighty influ-
> ence in the earth and among the children of men. The Lord has
> laid out much for thee to do. He has designed thee to be a wise
> *counselor* and one who will be looked up to by thousands of thy
> fellows. (italics added)

The calling of counselor was again stressed in a second patriarchal blessing given by her father in 1939, early in her tenure as a
supervisor of teachers in the BYU Training School.

> . . . the Lord has blessed you with wonderful influence among
> your associates. I know that they love you and honor you not only
> for your *counsel* and advice but for your example which you have
> set. Through faithfulness and prayerfulness [your] influence will
> grow until many will bless your name and memory. (italics
> added)

Achieving this goal was difficult. Happily married to a very
young bishop while living on a farm in Highland, Utah, and then
helping and seeing him become a promising high school teacher,
Lillian was suddenly stricken, as her Grandmother Clayson had been,
by the death of her young husband in the spring of 1927. Faced with
the necessity of raising a son and daughter on her own, she developed
a fierce independence and determination to avoid being a widow
obligated to other people. During the Depression, she emphatically
told her children, "We will not accept welfare."

Her only choice for mere survival at age thirty-three was to return
to teaching at Harrington Elementary School in American Fork. (She
had previously taught for three years, from 1918 to 1924, in Provo,
supporting the family while her husband completed his B.A. degree.)
In her distress, Lillian did not yet realize she was already becoming

that rare kind of person who knows how to *listen* to another's problems and then to manage the task of counseling without controlling.

It was clear to everyone that she was a teacher of teachers. In 1928, just after her mother died, she received an invitation to move to Provo to teach in the BYU Training School. She took a different option and combined the two bereaved families—her own and her father's. By doing this, she helped her father realize his goal of a BYU bachelor's degree for each of his four youngest children. As usual, the needs of others determined her choices.

That concern for others, combined with her great skill as a moderator of conflict, made Lillian so effective that she was soon chosen to be principal of the Harrington School, where she remained until 1937. She was one of the first women chosen to be a school principal in the state of Utah.

She might have been content with her demanding life as single parent, as principal, and as church worker. But she was not. She decided to obtain her B.A. degree. Year after year, she traveled on the Bamberger Electric, the interurban train, to Provo to earn credits toward the degree. She later reported that in 1940, when she was finally going to receive her B.A., someone said to her, "At your age, are you going to march across the stage to get your diploma?" "I said, 'Indeed I am. I've worked for twenty-five years to get it.' And I did march as proudly as those students who were twenty years old." Eventually, she earned a master's degree as well.

No doubt the struggles and fatigues of those years contributed to her success when, in 1945, she was promoted at BYU to the position of Counselor of Women. Lillian succeeded wonderfully, according to just about every definition except receiving high pay.

Perhaps most remarkable was her gift for sympathetic listening and wise advice that transforms troubled lives. Many students who were plagued by poverty or bereavement have reported later that it was Lillian Booth who made it possible for them to continue.

Lillian's education didn't stop after her master's degree. In 1957 she spent several months with her son's family in London and France. Before leaving home, she was asked to represent the United States at

the 50th Jubilee of the British Federation of University Women
Celebration and was presented to Queen Elizabeth. On this trip, she
also studied at the Senate House, University of London, and the
British Museum. Lillian had always been active on the local, state,
and national levels of the American Association of University Women
beginning in 1944, having served as president of the Provo branch
and as state vice-president, at which time she organized nine new state
branches. She represented BYU at many conventions throughout the
United States and abroad.

Although she suffered many trials, Lillian never lost her sense of
humor. She found fun and good humor in small things and often
shared pranks and jokes with her six grandchildren. In 1959, when
she brought her new husband, Dr. Ray J. Davis, to stay with her
daughter's family, her two grandsons short-sheeted their bed. She
knew how to laugh when the joke was on her, but then she could later
pull similar jokes on the perpetrators.

As Counselor of Women at BYU, she was in reality Dean of
Women, and it sometimes troubled her that she was not given a title
comparable to her almost unbelievably demanding and diverse duties.
For someone with her passion for perfection, the job was indeed mon-
umental. The only time she complained about any lack of appreciation was on one occasion when a student had criticized her for not visiting her dormitory. Slightly piqued at the unfairness of the criticism,
she wrote the dean as follows:

> I should perhaps advertise my wares a little more and shout a
> little louder. Last year I visited all houses and dormitories three or
> four times and some many more (probably not a requirement of a
> dean).
>
> My job seems to be a job where no one knows exactly what a
> person does. Most weeks, besides being at school from 9:00 a.m.
> until 5:00 or 6:00 p.m. and having from twelve to twenty consul-
> tations daily, I spend two, three, and sometimes four nights each
> week until 10:00 to 12:00 on student activities. Last Monday
> night I was with a group from 5:00 p.m. until midnight in Salt
> Lake City. I also sponsored a large group Friday night. This week
> I spent Tuesday evening with a school group. This Friday about

forty girls who do not have homes here in Provo are having an initiation at my home.

Seldom a week passes that either parents or students are not at my home on school problems.

On one Thanksgiving at her house, she spent a long time with a troubled girl while our family and invited guests finally ate without her. This kind of incident happened on numerous holidays.

Lillian's activities at BYU were strenuous. Nevertheless, she succeeded in being a good homemaker and mother. Her modest home was always clean, orderly, and furnished in good taste, and she was vitally concerned about her children's education and behavior. Though she may have started the day at 5:00 a.m., if her daughter, Lucille, was out on a date in the evening, Lillian would stay up until she returned—then if she wanted to talk, Lillian again became a good listener and confidante.

Lillian was a popular speaker in Utah and Idaho, and she enjoyed a number of honors. Among other recognitions, she served as president of BYU Women and of Idaho State Faculty Women (at age seventy) and was listed in Who's Who in Education in 1948. Her church activities included serving in the presidency of ward and stake MIA organizations and in the Primary. Nationally, she was recognized as Dean of Women and was invited to be panel chair of the National Dean of Women's Convention in San Francisco, California.

The true measure of success as a dean or counselor is, of course, what happens to those who are counseled. In 1991, Lillian's daughter, Lucille, was giving a Relief Society lesson about service, in which her son, Wayne, talked briefly, without mentioning her name, about a woman he knew who exemplified those virtues. Someone in the group said, "That was your mother, wasn't it?" and immediately the meeting had turned into a testimonial to Lillian Booth, with woman after woman relating experiences about how she had helped them and their families with their problems. Never one to define an assignment narrowly, Lillian found herself counseling young men as well as young women, serving as a mother figure to them—something the male deans could hardly provide. She was especially helpful to young widows who needed her comfort and advice in their bereavement.

One of her counseling principles was often expressed to her children: "If you feel you have enemies, the way to get rid of them is to turn them into your friends." Although this principle never led her to an easy tolerance of misbehavior, it also never resulted in a rejection of a person because of immoral deeds.

Once she befriended an elementary student who left her threatening notes with lipstick (blood) fingerprints on them. When the child was discovered, she said she hated all people in authority. Lillian became her friend, and the girl still wrote regularly until Lillian's death. On another occasion, Lillian was assigned to keep track of a member of the Pachuco gang, who came to BYU from California. This young woman had been involved in many questionable activities, but when she left BYU to marry a returned missionary, Lillian lent her money. From then on she heard from her regularly, the first letter containing a repayment of the loan.

When Lillian resigned her position in 1959 at age sixty-four to marry Ray J. Davis, chair of the Botany Department at Idaho State University, she turned once again to the roles of wife and stepmother to four sons. She traveled the world, camping along a path from Mexico through the United States to Canada, following blooming spring wildflowers with her husband who was writing a book. She and her family were flooded with expressions of regret at her early retirement but full of gratitude for the way in which she had treated each student's problems almost as if they were her own. Many colleagues have reported that their own methods of counseling were influenced by Lillian's example.

Her death on March 21, 1967, came from a sudden heart attack at the end of her world tour. She had only been home for five days. During that five-day period she exhibited smiling courage and even good humor. She had lived a steadfast, honorable, and unselfish life and had nothing to regret and nothing to fear. She faced death without complaint or self-pity. Those who saw her at the end felt, as all who had known her knew, that she was indeed a great woman. Her life of aspiration, courage, love, and charity was fulfilled.

Janet Calder
President's Office
by
Jan Nelson Ekeroth

Always cheerful and concerned for the needs of others, Janet Calder, executive secretary to the president, is one of BYU's best-kept secrets.

It is an understatement to say that many people have many opinions on many subjects when it comes to BYU, but there would be unanimous opinion on Janet Calder—that she is the sweetest, kindest person imaginable in her position. The fact that for more than twenty years she has helped four university presidents with every kind of personal or professional problem is a tribute to her and to the university she loves so much."

These words from Elder Jeffrey R. Holland perfectly describe Janet Calder, now executive secretary to President Merrill J. Bateman. Elder Dallin H. Oaks, eighth president of Brigham Young University has similar praise:

"Early in my service at BYU, I appointed two people who have continued to serve and who have had an enormous impact for good on BYU and its people. I consider the appointment of these two persons among the very most important things I did during my years at BYU. One is Coach LaVell Edwards. The other is Janet Calder."

Other BYU alumnae may have gained greater public acclaim or national exposure, but nobody's blood runs as blue—Cougar Blue— as Janet Calder's. Born in Provo, Utah, on December 11, 1940, Janet is the daughter of J. Hamilton (deceased) and Myrtle Iverson Calder. She has one brother, James, and is very close to him and his wife, Ann Christopherson Calder. Although she has not married and had children of her own, "Aunt Janet" is truly a second mother to Jim and Ann's six children: Jay, Christine, Catherine, Mark, Kimberly, and Scott Calder.

Janet's attitude about her life as a single woman is part of what draws others to her. She relates the following experience:

Several months ago, I ran into a former classmate whom I hadn't seen since high school. We were surprised to discover that our lives had taken similar turns. Neither of us had married nor had children, but we had both continued our education beyond high school and had found interesting employment. As we parted, my friend said to me, "My childhood dreams didn't come true, and I feel I have led a wasted life. I'm nothing but a failure." I couldn't believe what I was hearing! My first impulse was to shake her by the shoulders and shout, "No, you are not a failure! Perhaps your life took a different direction than you thought it would, but don't let that discourage you!" However, because we were both in a hurry, I said nothing.

Since then, my mind has returned to that conversation again and again. Each time I find myself wondering why my friend has a different outlook on life than I do. Like my friend, my childhood dreams haven't been fulfilled either, but why is it that she feels like a failure and I don't?

I know my membership in the Church has given me strength to face every situation, and it also gives me comfort and hope for the future. In addition, significant people in my life have shared their keys to happiness with me. They have taught me by their examples that, in spite of life's challenges and disappointments, we are here to be happy. And happiness comes from looking outward instead of inward, from working hard, and from serving others.

Janet's positive perspective on life is captured in some of her favorite sayings and mottos. She may be heard saying, "Life is an adventure," or, "Life is too short to be little," or, "Happiness is not a destination, but a journey." And one of her favorite scriptures reiterates her attitudes: "This is the day which the Lord hath made; we will rejoice and be glad in it" (Psalm 118:24).

After graduating from Provo High School in 1959, Janet entered the Executive Assistant Program at Brigham Young University. With her fine mind, balanced outlook, and gift for making friends, Janet was well equipped for her chosen field. During her years as a BYU student, Janet took time out of her studies to be a member of the Phi Chi Theta business club and a treasurer of the Val Norn social unit.

In 1963, after graduating with a bachelor's from the College of Business, Janet embarked on one of four trips she would take to Europe. Upon her return, she continued taking classes at BYU and in 1964 began working full time for Dean Antone K. Romney of BYU's College of Education. It was this experience that convinced Janet to qualify herself as a teacher. Although she taught only one year at Salt Lake's Olympus High School, Janet has continued to recertify as a teacher for twenty-five years, often taking rare vacation days to attend seminars and classes at BYU.

It was perhaps Dean Antone Romney who taught Janet one of her most valuable lessons. One day while taking minutes in a confidential meeting, Janet voiced her concern to Dean Romney about the content of the meeting. "You'd probably prefer that I keep my ears closed, wouldn't you?" With a teasing glint in his eye, Dean Romney replied, "You can keep your ears open but keep your damn mouth shut." Janet has always been more of a listener than a talker, but this order had its impact: to this day there is no one who can keep a confidence better than Janet Calder.

In 1971, when the newly appointed BYU president, Dallin H. Oaks, began his search for a secretary, Janet's name was mentioned. Working at that time at the University of Utah, Janet had no plans to return to Provo—that is, until she was introduced to President Oaks. Following her interview, Janet admitted to her mother, "I've had the most wonderful hour of my life visiting with President Oaks, but I'll never get the job." Humble and unassuming, Janet began her remarkable service in the BYU President's Office on August 26, 1971.

No training manual could prepare someone for the constant questions, callers, and visitors that find their way to the President's Office. Janet's greatest strengths are her love for people, her sympathetic nature, and her endless patience. In equal measure, she is able to empathize with a distraught parent, remain calm with the angriest student, and listen intently to a talkative caller. And it is not unusual to find on Janet's desk a token of esteem from a chagrined student or someone she has assisted. "Janet had to say 'no' to a lot of people," says Elder Oaks. "I never ceased to be amazed at how she could do that so skillfully that people seemed to be happier to hear 'no' from her than 'yes' from anyone else."

Sensitive, tenderhearted, and intensely loyal, Janet has emotions that run very deep. After nine years of a particularly close relationship with the Oaks family, she was overwhelmed with a sense of helplessness and devastation when, while in Singapore on a tour, she learned of President Oaks's resignation from BYU.

Although Jeffrey R. Holland, ninth president of BYU, was quick to reassure Janet that she had a job with him, she decided to take time away from the President's Office to become a secretary to William Rolfe Kerr, who was leaving as president of Dixie College to serve as executive vice-president in the Holland administration. It proved to be a choice experience for both of them.

"Janet's work was guided by a sense of absolute integrity," writes Elder Kerr, "with a never-ending desire to do everything within her capacity to facilitate the effectiveness of our office and of the university. Her stamp will be an indelible imprint on Brigham Young University in years to come. She would be the last to seek public recognition, but she should be the first to receive it."

Three short years after having left the President's Office, President Holland asked Janet to return when her former position became vacant. Calling her absolutely guileless, Elder Holland writes, "Janet is purely and truly one of the gentlest people I have ever known. On any given day in the President's Office, personal inquiries and sensitive circumstances might originate with the newest student on campus, the most seasoned faculty member, a concerned parent, or the national news media—but Janet could handle them all. Whatever the subject and whoever the visitor, she received each with graciousness, courtesy, and a genuine sense of helpfulness."

Janet is meticulous, methodical, and always prepared. Her penchant for order led Elder Holland to tell the following story. (He laughs even now when he recalls it.) One night he was working late and needed to get into Janet's desk. Rifling through pencils and notepads, he accidentally found a note she had written to herself about the Hollands' Christmas gift giving—a matter of personal difficulty for Janet.

No amount of encouragement from Janet in early October could get President Holland rolling on gifts any earlier than Christmas Eve. Without fail, he would come into the office on December 24 loaded down with gifts, and every year, he would ask Janet in a last-minute rush to help him get them to his administrators. This particular year, Janet, in an effort to help herself be patient and autonomous, wrote this note: "President Holland never wants to make a decision about Christmas gifts until Christmas is here. He doesn't want to deal with it, so just forget any reminders. He's never going to want to do it early, and I just have to realize that I have to manage the Christmas gifts myself."

President Holland burst into laughter because the note was such an accurate description of himself and the annual Christmas frenzy—and an equally accurate insight into Janet's "little red hen" desire for efficiency and cooperation, but eventual acceptance of the necessity of doing things herself. When he showed it to Janet the next day, she turned as red as a University of Utah sweatshirt, but the embarrassment was quickly forgotten as they both broke into laughter at the absolute truthfulness of the message. In an administration marked by many humorous moments, this was one of their favorite private jokes.

No position is more precarious than a secretarial slot on the third floor of the Smoot Administration Building, and in 1989 Janet was faced again with uncertainty when President Holland was called to the First Quorum of Seventy. It was clear early on, however, that his successor, Rex E. Lee, had no intention of losing such a valuable asset. President Lee notes:

"Customarily, universities have no established official diplomatic or protocol offices, such as the Departments of State or Foreign Ministries on which sovereign nations rely. Brigham Young University, nevertheless, has such an office as a de facto matter. The officer operates without appropriate title, but no one who has ever dealt with her has any doubt that she is in fact in charge of a large segment of BYU's diplomatic relations.

"Over my years in government, I came in contact with many diplomats and other people who were skilled in matters of diplomacy. Many of those people, trained for the task and highly experienced, were very good. But I have never seen anyone who can match our own BYU Secretary of State, Janet Calder."

Since President Lee's recent death, Janet continues to serve in her post as "Secretary of State" in President Merrill J. Bateman's administration. Her loyalty has now extended to four BYU presidents, and her sensitive and devoted contributions to BYU are immeasurable. Some employees are content just to put in their time at BYU. But for Janet Calder that is not enough. She has given Brigham Young University no less than her heart.

Kathryn Basset Pardoe
Pioneering Dramatist

by

Shannon Keeley

Kathryn Basset Pardoe taught in BYU's Speech and Drama Department—a department she founded with her husband, Earl— while raising five children. At times during her almost fifty years with the department, she was expected to run the department alone in Earl's absence. Among her countless other productions and performances, Kathryn became well known in the 1930s for her role as Mary, mother of Christ, in the BYU productions of Family Portrait. The information for this sketch was taken from a Pardoe family history Kathryn wrote and a transcription of her oral history.

*A*s the stage lights dim, the audience sits back in plush violet chairs and waits for heavy curtains to part and actors to give voice to a once speechless script. The performers cast their words—spoken and sung—out into the spacious auditorium. Perhaps tonight's actors will receive a standing ovation. When the performance is over, the audience will file out of the theater, the actors will disperse, and the Pardoe Theater will be empty, dark, and quiet. Or will it?

For those who knew the people whose name the theater bears, a voice still hovers over the stage even when the seats are empty: the voice of Kathryn Basset Pardoe. The Pardoe name is easy to overlook, but each ticket stub with the Pardoe name on it is a memorial to this remarkable woman.

Kathryn Basset's voice sounded through auditoriums long before she became a Pardoe. She was born on August 24, 1892, and it was not long before her talents began to emerge. In fact, she played her first starring role in kindergarten as "Little Robin Red Breast" and later read "The Hazing of the Valiant" at her eighth-grade graduation exercises. Both her parents were fond of the theater and took Kathryn and her brother to community theatrical events when she was young. But more often than not, Kathryn found a way to be on the stage rather than in the audience—singing with the ward choir, for example, led to three years in the Tabernacle Choir.

While Kathryn's father attended each of her performances and listened to her clear voice, he himself fought a handicap in the art of vocal delivery: a severe speech impediment. He had always been promised by ecclesiastical leaders that he would someday overcome the burden of his impediment, but he wrestled with his stammering for most of Kathryn's childhood. He visited speech therapists and church leaders, but nothing changed.

One night Mr. Basset gathered Kathryn and the other children around his bed and prayed, asking the Lord what more he could do to overcome his handicap. The next morning he casually remarked that he felt better, and he never stammered again. After overcoming his own handicap, he spent innumerable hours helping others with similar speech problems, eventually opening a school of speech therapy. Mr. Basset's steady new voice was the product of more than speech therapy—it was a gift from the Lord and a sign to Kathryn that her voice was a gift as well.

Kathryn's voice quickly became a commodity in high demand. During her first year of school in Logan, Utah, President Dalby of Ricks Academy in Idaho asked Kathryn to teach English and speech there the following school year. At first she declined, reminding him that she had not yet graduated from high school. But President Dalby insisted she was qualified and persuaded her to accept the job. So Kathryn taught during the school year, and in the summer, she performed readings and sang in duets with a tour group that traveled for six weeks across Idaho, Washington, and Oregon.

A few years later, in 1913, the principal of Central Junior High School in Ogden, Utah, asked Kathryn to take a position teaching English and speech. Having just finished some courses at Henniger Business School, she had intended to leave Ogden for a job in Salt Lake City. Kathryn declined the job at first; she still had not officially graduated from high school and did not deem herself qualified. Intent on hiring her, the principal persuaded her to accept the job.

Her decision to remain in Ogden for that teaching position proved to be a wise choice since that was where she met her husband, Earl Thomas Pardoe. At the time, Earl was due in New York to begin rehearsing for a production of *The Student Prince*, so he had intended to remain in Ogden for only a week and a half. He soon abandoned his plans when he met Kathryn, whom his sister Leah had invited to dinner. Earl proposed marriage on their third date, but Kathryn turned him down because she still had attachments to a boyfriend on a mission. But after praying and thinking more about Earl's proposal, Kathryn changed her mind and decided to marry him, a decision that began the union of two of the most talented dramatists in LDS history. Earl sacrificed his major role in The Student Prince and opened a drama studio in Ogden. Kathryn continued to teach at Central Junior High and signed up at the studio as Earl's first student. During their time in Ogden, one of Kathryn's leading roles was Ruth Richards in *The Daughter of a Pioneer*, directed by her husband in 1915.

In 1919, Earl and Kathryn left Ogden to develop a speech and drama department at BYU. By that time Kathryn had William, Norma, and the newborn Catherine to care for, but as soon as she reached BYU, she enrolled in classes to finish her high-school diploma. To meet house payments, Kathryn and Earl furnished and rented out the bedrooms in their basement to six college boys, one of whom was Ernest Wilkinson, later president of BYU. Kathryn not only kept up the home, but cooked dinner for these boys. Still, she managed to quickly fulfill her graduation requirements, and the next fall she began teaching classes at BYU with Earl.

Kathryn and Earl had eleven students in their first theater class, but they faced a major dilemma—they had no theater. Because the local Columbia theater was too expensive to rent, President Brimhall put the Pardoes in charge of adapting the old College Hall into a theater. The hall was nothing more than an auditorium, but Kathryn and Earl, with the help of some young men, worked tirelessly to transform it into a theater. They remodeled the entire building by ripping out the floors, installing new chairs, building a new stage and constructing suitable scenery. The final product was primitive, but the Pardoes worked through the rough spots and produced a major play nearly every month.

After completing that project, Kathryn and Earl converted an empty classroom into another theater by building a stage and proscenium opening. They used that room to produce one-act plays and to help students direct their own theatrical productions. In addition to helping her husband build these new theaters and teaching classes at the university, Kathryn also took more classes and cared for her growing family. By 1922 they had four children, and Kathryn still found time to teach English at Provo High School during the mornings.

Earl left Provo for two years to pursue a master's degree at Columbia University, and Kathryn remained at BYU, running the department in Earl's absence and singlehandedly taking care of their family. During that time she put on *The First Year, Smiling Through,* and the opera *The Gondoliers.* As challenging as these productions were and as busy as Kathryn's schedule was, she claimed that directing was an easy task compared to completing her chemistry course. It wasn't until after Earl returned home from Columbia that Kathryn was able to complete her own college degree. She had already been teaching at the university level for six years.

In the years that followed, Kathryn and Earl moved to California where Earl founded and taught at the Department of Corrective Speech at the University of Southern California. Always involved in a number of projects, Kathryn wrote book reviews for the library in Long Beach, and in 1932 signed a contract to perform sixteen interpretive readings for the local Ebell and Friday Morning Clubs.

That same year, the new BYU president, Dr. Franklin Harris, requested that the Pardoes return to BYU. Kathryn and Earl let their children decide whether they should stay in California or go back to Utah. When they chose Utah, Kathryn cancelled her contract, and the family returned in 1933 with the promise of teaching positions for both Kathryn and Earl. Not long after they settled back in Provo, however, Earl left again to pursue his doctoral degree at Louisiana State University, and once again, the teaching fell solely to Kathryn. But even with that heavy responsibility, it was not until 1944 that Kathryn was finally put on the official payroll of BYU and given her own salary. By that time she had been teaching at the university twenty-five years.

Kathryn also continued acting. She played the role of Mary, the mother of Christ, in *Family Portrait*, which was produced every Christmas season for eight years. It is said that she requested the university cease producing the play because people were stopping her on the street to tell her she *was* Mary. In 1938, Kathryn was appointed to the YWMIA board where she served just shy of ten years.

A few years after Earl completed his doctorate, the Pardoes experienced a string of hardships. Their youngest son David died in an accident on a scouting trip, and Kathryn's mother, who had been living with them, died thirteen weeks later. Within a short time, the remaining four children, Thomas Jr., Norma, William, and Catherine, left the Pardoe nest one by one to marry, serve in the military, or pursue careers. Kathryn and Earl found themselves alone. Their once bustling household was now still, and Kathryn was lonely. Not only was their son Tom fighting in World War II, but a number of Kathryn and Earl's former students had also been drafted. To stave off loneliness, they wrote letters to those boys; for some it was the only mail they received. Sometimes two or three "clothes buckets" full of letters stood waiting by the Pardoe's front door to be mailed.

Even though Earl's teaching career ended in 1950, and he had left Kathryn again to serve a mission in New England, Kathryn continued to teach in a drama department that had changed radically since the couple had founded it. New professors with new ideas had joined the department, and Kathryn sometimes found her voice being drowned out. She had to speak louder and stronger, not only to hold her ground at the university, but to compensate for the loss of her eyesight. While Earl was still in New England, Kathryn began suffering from painful spasms in her eyes. By the time the doctors diagnosed the problem as glaucoma, it was too late to begin treatment. She underwent a series of operations on both eyes, but continued to lose her sight.

When Earl returned from his mission, he went to work for the Alumni House, organizing the records of graduated students. Kathryn continued to teach until she retired in 1968. Even after retirement, she kept busy giving monodramas, such as *Fanny, Waters of the Moon*, and portions of *Family Portrait*. Kathryn and Earl traveled extensively throughout Europe and took groups of colleagues on organized tours.

In October of 1971, after Earl decided he could no longer work, the faculty and alumni gave him an extravagant party in honor of all he had contributed to the university. Three weeks later, he died in Kathryn's arms as she was helping him from his bed to the restroom. After Earl's death, Kathryn lost her sight completely. She passed away ten years later.

It seems so simple now to file into the spacious Pardoe Theater and enjoy the excellent performances. Most people don't realize what went into the development of the drama program at BYU and the thankless jobs Kathryn performed, often in Earl's shadow or absence. Unlike Earl, Kathryn was never given a gala for her contributions to BYU. She spent her final years blind and suffering from arthritis in her body and hands—hands that once hammered nails into BYU's first theater; hands that wrote hundreds of letters to BYU students and chalked out assignments on blackboards; hands that held her husband as he took his final breaths. "Oh, I wish I had kept some sort of a diary," Kathryn wrote in her family history shortly before she died. Yet even though she didn't leave a diary behind, it seems she left something that, although somewhat faint, is just as good: the resonating legacy of a voice of her own.

Mary Anne Quinn Wood

J. Reuben Clark School of Law

compiled by

Marian W. Jensen

Mary Anne Quinn Wood, the first woman law professor at Brigham Young University, is one of those attorneys who works persistently to accumulate and present accurate information and to adhere not only to the law, but to basic moral principles. She is one who has achieved remarkably in her profession and has still remained loyal to her Christian values. She has also raised a family of five children.

*M*ary Anne and Stephen Wood drove to 47 E. South Temple in Salt Lake City, Utah, to keep their appointment with Elder Marion G. Romney, the interview with a General Authority that is required of all prospective faculty members at Church schools. They were apprehensive because of Mary Anne's unique role—a role very different from that of the traditional stay-at-home LDS woman. Elder Romney soon dissipated their fears and gave full approval for Mary Anne and Stephen to teach at the J. Reuben Clark Law School together. Mary Anne was the first woman to receive such an appointment. But Elder Romney's approval came with something of a stipulation. His parting words of advice were: "Be good teachers, and have more children." The Woods have been true to his counsel, and Mary Anne has been highly influential in this pioneering appointment.

Mary Anne Quinn's life began in Washington, D.C., on February 20, 1945. She is the sixth of Horace Alford and Alice Badger Quinn's eight children. Since her father was a career military officer, the family moved around during much of her growing up. She was educated in northern Virginia and Greenwich, Connecticut, where she was not only an excellent student, but also active in extracurricular activities, including student government, athletics, and speech and debate.

Following her junior year of high school in 1962, Mary Anne enrolled at Brigham Young University. After her graduation in 1966 with a B.A. in English, she filled a mission for the LDS Church to the Central States Mission. Upon her release, Mary Anne immediately began her studies at the University of Utah Law School where she met Stephen Wood. The following year, 1967, the two were married. This marriage was the beginning of a remarkable partnership in which this couple has shared mutual interests, a desire to support one another, and a commitment to their Latter-day Saint convictions.

When Stephen graduated from the University of Utah Law School, Mary Anne accompanied him to New York City where he was a Jervey Fellow at the Columbia School of Law. He continued his graduate studies at the University of Munich, and during this time, Mary Anne gave birth to their first child, Emily. Stephen was subsequently awarded a doctorate in juridical science from Columbia University.

In 1972, after Stephen had obtained his academic credentials, which include an emphasis in international legal issues, the Woods moved to Washington, D.C., Mary Anne's "hometown." It was here that their second child, Mary Alice, was born. Caring for these two daughters was a joy, but Mary Anne could not ignore a compelling desire to complete what she had started at the University of Utah. She returned to law school at George Washington University, graduating in 1976, first in her class and with highest honors. Her own determined efforts accounted for much of her success, but Mary Anne could never have achieved what she did without her supportive husband. In fact, she recognizes that Stephen is always a chief player, not only in all their combined efforts, but also her individual achievements. She calls him a supreme mediator and diplomat, whether he is enlisting parental support for the Meridian School in Provo (which he helped found in 1989), hosting foreign dignitaries, or settling disputes at home.

With Mary Anne's graduation came some critical decisions. Where would they live and what direction would they take so they could both use their legal education and at the same time attend to the needs of their children? Ultimately, they felt that academic appointments would allow them more time and flexibility to care for their children than practicing in a traditional law firm. Thus, their appointments at the J. Reuben Clark Law School at Brigham Young University seemed the ideal solution.

Mary Anne and Stephen started their teaching with an energetic and conscientious attitude. Mary Anne has typically taught courses in contracts, while Stephen has continued his focus on international law. To the Woods' delight, Mary Anne gave birth to three more children—Stephen, Rachel, and Joseph—while teaching at the law school. These babies slept many hours in a crib in Mary Anne's BYU office during their first few months. Difficult as it must be, Mary Anne and Stephen have been remarkably successful over the years in alternating their schedules and coordinating their efforts so that they have been able to raise their children and at the same time teach and progress at the law school.

Since Mary Anne's appointment at BYU, she has had a number of other career opportunities. In 1981, she was selected as a White

House Fellow and served as special assistant to Casper Weinberger, Secretary of Defense, for one year. Following her fellowship, she and her family returned to Provo where her husband resumed his position as a full-time law professor while Mary Anne commenced practicing with the firm of Holme, Roberts & Owen, in addition to teaching part time at BYU.

Later, in 1990, Mary Anne Wood formed her own law firm. Wood Spendlove & Quinn is a firm engaging primarily in commercial litigation, real estate, and employment law. It was retained in 1991 to represent the State of Utah in the ACLU's challenge of the state's abortion law and successfully defended seven of the nine provisions attacked as unconstitutional. Mary Anne regards the preparation and presentation of that case as her most significant professional contribution to date. This impressive victory was the result of years of work and an undeviating belief that her cause was just and moral. In 1994, when Utah's attorney general tried to eliminate her work and efforts, the governor, Michael Leavitt, intervened, stating with fervor that Mrs. Wood's legal work and findings were too valuable to the State of Utah to be eliminated.

While her work with the abortion issue is the one that has captured the front page of local newspapers, Mary Anne has also been involved in many other valuable projects. She has served on many boards including the board of trustees of Utah Valley State College, the Utah State Constitutional Revision Commission, the Governor's Task Force on the Utah Anti-Discrimination Division, and the Executive Committee of the Thrasher Research Fund, a charitable trust administered by the LDS Church. She has also prepared materials on the American Disability Act and its application in Utah.

With her many professional, family, and community accomplishments, most marvel at how Mary Anne is able to accomplish so much. To begin with, she typically gets up at five a.m. and then retires late. But she is also obviously possessed with a remarkable drive and determination, qualities that she recognizes probably come from her pioneer ancestors. In fact, Mary Anne has always been very proud of her Mormon pioneer heritage and tries to live in keeping with that legacy.

One ancestor, for example, was Rodney Badger, a scout for Brigham Young. Another, from South Africa, became a member of a handcart company. And many were impoverished immigrants from England who worked hard to establish themselves among the Saints in a new land. Mary Anne is particularly proud of her foremothers who helped settle the Utah territory, raising and educating large families, often on their own. Her paternal grandmother was an early Utah businesswoman who also ran for governor in the early 1930s. And her maternal grandfather was one of the first Utahns to go to Washington, D.C., with Senator Smoot; he served as Senator Smoot's secretary while attending law school at George Washington University. Mary Anne identifies with this grandfather for several reasons: he graduated from George Washington Law School seventy years before Mary Anne did, and Mary Anne started her own firm in the same building where his law offices were located sixty years ago.

Continuing the faithful legacy of her pioneer ancestors, Mary Anne has been active in the LDS Church from her youth, serving in the auxiliaries of the Church wherever she has lived. In particular, she has taught adult Sunday School and Relief Society Spiritual Living lessons for more than twenty years.

Though busy in their Church and professional lives, Mary Anne and Stephen also take time for recreation with their family. But even Mary Anne's leisure activities can be serious business. She has completed several local triathlons, a rigorous athletic event consisting of a one-mile swim, a twenty-five-mile bike ride, and a six-mile run. Mary Anne also enjoys mountain biking with her husband (and as many of their five children as can be persuaded), snow skiing, visiting the national parks in and out of state, and four-wheeling.

Amid the incredible diversity and activity in the Wood's lives, their unity and conviction as wife and husband have resulted in a remarkable team effort; Mary Anne and Stephen have successfully reared a family and have contributed significantly to Brigham Young University, their legal professions, and their community.

Anna Boss Hart

College of Education

contributed by

John Hart

Aside from Anna Hart's remarkable teaching ability and her gift for inspiring prospective teachers, she was also a mother to her son, John, and a member of the Relief Society General Board for many years. John Hart responded to inquiries about his mother with appreciation and a generous supply of material about her. The three items selected for this sketch give unusual insight into one of BYU's great women.

*T*his biographical sketch appeared in the Relief Society Magazine, March 1940:

Anna Boss Hart, daughter of Adolph Boss and Sara Alleman, received her Bachelor of Arts degree from Utah State University. She then served an LDS mission to Texas. Her marriage to John William Hart, the eminent Senator in Idaho, was prematurely shortened by his sudden death seven months before their son, John, was born. After this, Sister Hart studied at the University of Utah and the University of Wisconsin, receiving her M.A. from the University of Southern California.

In 1940, a year after beginning work at BYU, she was called to the Relief Society General Board and served in that capacity for twenty-nine years.

Asked to define her education, Anna Boss Hart said, "Education is service to life and to eternity." Through the decades of her career, over six thousand students have been affected by her teaching ideals. "I teach them to want the right kind of happiness, and they succeed on their own." Once asked to list her many accomplishments, Anna said, "I am my students. When they hurt, I hurt. When they succeed, I am grateful."

In 1965, sixty alumni of BY High School commissioned a portrait of her and donated it to BYU before she retired in August, 1973. Anna spent twenty-six of her thirty-seven years teaching at BY High School, where she taught the fundamentals of life through literature and the discipline of writing.

Sister Anna Hart feels a great appreciation for the life and inspiration of her mother, husband, son, relatives, friends, and her Church. Unquestioned loyalty and support has characterized all her activities.

Tucked in with the other material John Hart sent was the follow-ing note from his wife, Shauna:

John and I married after his mother died, so I did not have the opportunity to meet her. I have read her biography and have heard stories and comments about her, including John's own memories, so I feel I know and love her.

However, if I had never read or heard anything about Anna B., I would always be grateful to her for the way she raised her only son. I know some of the characteristics he has came from her: his gentle consideration and unselfish attitude toward others, his patience, his efficiency and proficiency, and his desire to serve others.

Since being married to a living legacy of hers, I can only add my appreciation for this remarkable woman.

Another excerpt comes from the Daily Universe, *Friday, October 11, 1991. Written by Mary E. Lee, it won first place in a student essay contest.*

It was a warm afternoon in May. We had moved into an empty old house at 293 East 600 North. Initially I had wanted to take up the carpet and refinish the hardwood floor underneath. Then I remembered that the baby would be here soon and possibly crawling by the winter months. The floor would be too cold for little knees. Besides, the landlord probably wouldn't allow it—this was the house he grew up in, and when we signed the contract he made it clear that he wouldn't allow it—that he only wanted renters that would maintain his boyhood home with care. Radical changes were out of the question.

I was hoping, however, that he would allow one small change which I was sure that anyone in their right mind would allow. There were, by my count, seventy-three built-in shelves in the house—shelves were everywhere. I didn't mind them, except for those in the bedroom. Surely our landlord would be reasonable enough to allow us to tear out some of the shelves in order to make more room for a bed.

My inquiry met with disappointment. The shelves were part of the house and they were to stay—end of discussion.

My newlywed decorating dilemma was quickly dismissed as the baby came and life was swept away into a sea of new emotions, smells, and sensations. Visitors streamed through our home to see our little blessing.

One visitor in particular, Carma DeJong Anderson, was thrilled with the baby, but equally thrilled with our home.

After the baby went to sleep and we had slipped out of the nursery into the living room, Carma exclaimed, "Do you know whose home you are living in?" The question was obviously rhetorical because she allowed no opportunity for me to answer. "Anna Boss Hart's," she said, "a great lady. She taught at BY High just up the street, as well as at BYU. She was the most influential teacher in my life. She died just a few years ago—she was a great woman."

Those were the first words I heard of Anna Boss Hart. She came to live with me the day we were introduced.

My mind was constantly on her as I went about my daily tasks. This was once a great woman's home and I was a poor replacement for a great woman, no matter how hard I tried.

She stood by me as I bathed my baby. She watched me dig in her flower bed. She knelt by my side as I scrubbed her floors on my hands and knees, and I felt her eye upon me as I replaced the wallpaper in her bathroom. But mostly, she observed when I dusted all those shelves.

At first, I wanted to ask her why she was so crazy to build so many shelves in such a small house. My questions soon took a different form as I felt her quiet influence. I knew full well that her treasures were books.

My curiosity eventually focused upon my small collection of books. I hadn't read many of them. Though I had neglected them, they sat patiently waiting for my attention.

They seemed willing to wait a lifetime for me. Luckily, they didn't have to because something, maybe a quiet nudge from Anna, coaxed me to pick up one and not just dust it, but open it up and start reading.

That day, I rediscovered a childhood sweetheart of sorts. Memories of many hours spent lost in a world of books came flooding back to me.

I am studying English literature at BYU right now, so the books are pouring in almost on a daily basis. Anna comes to visit from time to time, but not to see me. I get the feeling that she sees her work with me as completed. She launched me in a direction which has already brought much joy to my home.

You see, I have a two-year-old daughter who can barely reach the shelves in her own bedroom, where we keep her small collection of books. Sometimes I think Anna gives her a boost up while she strains to reach her books. My latest concern is, when we move away, will we find a house with shelves enough to hold all of our books?

Anna Hart's BYU assignment was twofold: she taught English, especially her love of literature, to BY High School students, and she supervised the activities of senior BYU college students who were doing their student teaching in the field of English. This she did with enthusiasm and with a great personal interest in each prospective teacher. She provided them with materials and made them feel they could not fail.

Busy with her teaching and Relief Society General Board assignment, Anna had little time for much else, except to rear her only son, John. She not only encouraged him to be an excellent student, but also recognized that he needed athletic enjoyment. On one occasion, Anna climbed with John and one of his friends to the top of Mount Timpanogos. On the way down, they decided to slide down a glacier, a frightening experience for anyone. But to Anna, looking down the glacier, it was terrifying. Still, with her characteristic determination, she made the slide with John and his friend cheering her on. It was the thrill of a lifetime. After John married, Anna continued to teach until her retirement in 1973. She then served a mission in Berne, Switzerland.

Her associates knew her as one who always spoke well of others and every situation. "Nay, speak no ill" must have been one of her mottos. Her friends of the Provo Manavu Ward "family-home-evening group" became her substitute family after her son moved to California. At one of their gatherings, Marjorie Wight remembers that she sensed Anna was not feeling well. But Anna was never one to speak of any personal difficulties to anyone. In December 1980 her friends became aware that they had not seen her in a while. They learned that a nephew, who often checked on his aunt, discovered that she had quietly passed away in her bed, with a newspaper in hand, reading as she always did. Her passing marked the end of a great influence at BYU.

Beverly Lois Romney Cutler

College of Education

by

Joyce Cutler Stay

At the sudden death of her husband Robert, Beverly Cutler turned to her love of education—she went back to school for first a master's degree, then a doctorate in child development and early childhood education. She combined hard work, natural ability, and flexibility to help her cope with her difficulties, raise her family of five children, and build an outstanding academic career. The fruits of her many years of service to BYU, family, and the Church are impressive.

*W*hen Beverly Romney was attending a church gathering during her college years, she was introduced to Robert Garr Cutler, and something "clicked." They dated for a short period, getting to know one another as friends. Then during his two-year stint as an LDS missionary in Germany, the two frequently corresponded, and the friendship matured. After Robert returned in 1952, the couple was promptly married in the Salt Lake Temple by President Spencer W. Kimball. This has been a love affair from start to the present.

After their marriage, Robert continued his education at Princeton University where he obtained a Ph.D. in political science. He was then employed by the Office of Management and Budget in Washington, D.C. As their family grew, Beverly and Robert remained close and unified, with a free-flowing communication and similar goals. When their oldest child was only eight and the youngest, two, Robert suddenly passed away. Beverly was left to rear her five children—three daughters and two sons—alone.

Beverly was determined to overcome her adversity. She had done it before. Even as an infant, Beverly was a fighter. Shortly after she was brought home from the hospital as a newborn in December 1930, she had had to work to stay alive. Because of a serious case of whooping cough, she had to be placed near a source of warmth. But the coughing persisted. During this period of anxiety, her father and an uncle blessed her at home because they feared she might not survive long enough to attend the ward for this ordinance. Their anxiety yielded to gratitude when Beverly recovered from the illness.

Beverly's family had also known adversity. Vernon Romney, Beverly's father, had walked on crutches since childhood as a result of polio. His family had been forced to leave the Mormon colonies in Mexico because of the 1912 Mexican Civil War. When he finally settled in Utah, he had developed a passionate appreciation for the United States. Beverly inherited his independence, which in her has been tempered by a sweetness from her mother.

When Beverly and Robert married, neither of them sensed what was ahead of them. Although his unexpected death had been traumatic, Beverly's power to cope was remarkable. She explained to her children that Heavenly Father needed their father's services on the "other side." Friends and relatives came to her rescue with finances and support, and Beverly returned to school to obtain her master's degree from BYU. Then in 1966 she graduated with her doctorate at Stanford University in child development and early childhood education.

Beverly's love of education had begun many years before her husband's death. As a child, she had always loved school. By age thirteen, she would wake up at three in the morning to study in the breakfast room. She would sneak in, closing both doors so no one would see the light. Then she would try to creep back into bed just as it was beginning to get light—so her family wouldn't suspect anything. With her natural gifts and hard work, she earned A's in all her classes from first grade up through her last year at Stanford University.

But Beverly wasn't your typical bookworm. She developed in other areas as well. She has fond memories of family excursions, especially short trips to Zion's Park and Yellowstone. When Beverly was young, all ten Romneys traveled in an old Marmon (a small car) to see the San Francisco World's Fair. Later, in 1948, the family accompanied their father to Philadelphia for the National Republican Convention where he seconded the nomination of Senator Taft for president of the United States. As they traveled, they would eat their bottled fruit and vegetables brought from home. At night they would stay in motels. Because there were so many of them, they often had to sneak in or duck when driving by the office. Beverly remembers staying in a motel room where she, her mother, and her other three sisters had to lie sideways all night on one bed.

Without her unique background of survival, hard work, and adaptation (while having fun along the way), Beverly never would have been equipped as a single mother to tackle a Ph.D. When she was able to finish her doctorate, her first postgraduate position took her to the University of Alberta in Edmonton. There she set up her household and began supervising one of the first early childhood education programs in the area. Her work then led to the establishment of these programs throughout the province.

After three years of success in Canada, Beverly was recruited by BYU in 1969 and hired as an associate professor in the College of Education. One of her major contributions at BYU was the development of a class titled "Introduction to Learning and Teaching." This course, Elementary Education 310R, is required for all education majors. It places students in the public schools three to five days a week observing, learning, and giving brief lessons. Students learn the practical side of teaching to help them decide whether they really want to be teachers. Field experience of this type is found today in many other universities throughout the country. Her textbook, written specifically for this course, and an introductory text, *Teaching: An Introduction*, which Beverly co-authored, are used extensively in the United States and Canada. As the author of approximately fifty academic articles, she has traveled to many different countries to present her material.

Over the years, Beverly has been given additional assignments at BYU. One of her greatest delights has been the opportunity to teach occasional Book of Mormon and Doctrine and Covenants classes. She has also had a pioneering role in serving on various committees—on the University Women's Council and as chair of the University Curriculum Committee. Beverly served for a time on a Church-wide task force for higher education, and more recently as the associate dean of the College of Education.

Her colleagues have described her as one who is trustworthy, considerate, gracious, and has sound judgment. Quiet and unobtrusive, Beverly is an able administrator who doesn't sit behind a desk, calling people to her—she would rather go to them, listen to their ideas, and discuss. She has a delightful ability to always focus on the good in others.

Beverly's academic achievements are remarkable, but what do her children say of her? They marvel at her management skills, her ability to get along on only four to five hours of sleep a night, and her complete devotion to them as children when she was home. They remember that they consistently had regular family home evenings, even during the period when Beverly was working on her Ph.D. Saturday mornings were reserved for cleaning the home. As the children did their household tasks, they listened to classical music. Dusting and mopping didn't seem so dull when accompanied by a Mozart sonata or some Schubert songs.

Children are sometimes difficult to manage and Beverly's were no exception. Even gentle Beverly felt the impulse to spank at times. But the children recall these few instances as "love pats." Much more effective was one of Beverly's quick looks—then the children knew it was time to "shape up."

Sunday mornings were reserved for church. After Sunday dinner was over (which frequently included a pot roast—the meat for the entire week), the family would remain around the table for lengthy discussions about what they had learned at church, what was going on at school, or any problems they might be having. Because Beverly encouraged her children at an early age to plan for missions, the discussion sometimes centered around these plans. At times they would ask her about their deceased father, and she would recall her happy memories. Her love for him never died.

Beverly has brought a lot of the good times from her own childhood into her role as a mother. On special occasions she and the children would make their favorite dessert of homemade ice cream—peach, cherry, orange, or whatever fruit flavor was available. Their favorite vacation spot was a cabin on Bear Lake, owned by Beverly's father. While there, Beverly would sit outdoors and gaze at the sunset and the blue lake for hours on end, even though mosquitoes would buzz around her. She insisted that being inside, looking through the windows, wasn't good enough. She had to see everything.

During the past two decades Beverly has taken leave from BYU without pay to serve two full-time missions. In December 1982, she served a proselyting mission to Spain. Although she had studied some French during her early years in school, learning a new language—Spanish—was a challenge. Beverly applied herself with her usual diligence and learned to speak it well. She completed her mission with distinction and returned to BYU where she rejoined the faculty.

One Sunday morning in 1990, Beverly attended a stake conference where one of the speakers encouraged mature members of the church to volunteer for missionary service. She felt impressed to serve another mission and completed her application that week. Soon she and seven other members were called as the first LDS humanitarian missionaries in Romania. These eight pioneering spirits met in the MTC for a short period, but received no formal training in the language. Not until she arrived in Romania did Beverly, through intense self-study, learn to speak the difficult language with some facility.

As soon as the group arrived in Romania, she was able to see the country's desperate conditions. The angry Romanian people had just executed their communist dictator, Nicolae Ceausescu, and his family, and were still burning palace grounds. With almost nothing in the stores, Beverly and her missionary companions lived on a diet of cabbage, potatoes, and some occasional rice, which the mission president brought to them from outside the country.

Beverly was called to work with a number of orphanages and schools in Bucharest, the capital city of Romania. While there, she prepared a curriculum guide consisting of activities and reasonable goals for children through the third grade. The country's Ministry of Education received this publication with gratitude.

The first Romanian to be baptized in that country, Octavian Vasilescu, quietly told Beverly that her influence had initiated his desire to investigate the Church. Interest in the Church grew rapidly. When Beverly and her group returned to the United States, well over one hundred people were attending the LDS services in Romania. She considers her service in Romania one of the highlights of her life.

Now that her children are married, Beverly lives alone. But she always enjoys visiting with her grandchildren. On an occasional evening when she is free, Beverly finds delight in attending BYU productions—particularly of foreign films and classical music. Her love of music has been a constant in her life. The cello Beverly learned to play as a child has been handed down to her daughter, Carol, who has since played in several orchestras. As a great memorizer of hymns, Beverly loves to sing them with her family. Two of her favorites are "O, My Father" and "How Great Thou Art."

When Beverly retires in the summer of 1997, she would like to serve another mission, in addition to writing journals and family history. She says, "I am willing to take any experiences that may come along in my life." She believes that "all these things shall give experience." This is precisely the attitude that makes it seem that Beverly has already reached perfection. But her children assure us that, occasionally, she does have a human side. One of the few times they have heard her complain is in the spring of every year when she has to prepare her income tax.

Loved by her children and grandchildren, respected and trusted by her students and colleagues, Beverly Romney Cutler has lived a life of commitment to hard work and excellence. And her thoughtful consideration will live on as her family, friends, and students extend her influence into the lives of others.

Marie Tuttle

College of Education

by

Patricia Greaves, assisted by Ann Tuttle

Just as Anna Hart was a builder of teachers of the past and Beverly Cutler has been training teachers in the past and present, Marie Tuttle is preparing teachers for the future. Marie's unending enthusiasm, her willingness to assume responsibility, and her popularity with the students are just a few of the many traits that are establishing her outstanding reputation at Brigham Young University.

*G*randma Adamson was not one to mince words. When she learned that her granddaughter, Marie, was afraid to move from Spanish Fork to Las Vegas for her first teaching position, Grandma Adamson gave her some tart advice: "For hell's sake, girl, you're not going to fight the Indians!"

Perhaps these words were what pushed Marie forward. In 1969, she signed the teaching contract and packed her bags. At age twenty-two, just graduated from BYU, Marie left her close-knit family and hometown to face the world. The parting was a tearful one.

The second of Dean and Ann Adamson Tuttle's three children, Marie was born May 14, 1947. Even as a baby, her happy personality was evident. Those around her found a cheerfulness and determination in her that most of us only feel when May flowers begin to sprout.

Marie claims she grew up with a fishing pole in one hand and a paddle in the other. How she loved the family boat, the DeAnnMarLynn, named for each child: DeAnn, Marie, and Lynn! A favorite outing was to the family cabin at Strawberry Reservoir in northern Utah. Marie's dad loved having her go fishing with him because she always managed to catch fish. They would rise early so they could have the bait and fishing lines in the water before daybreak. It was a family joke that Marie frequently caught the most fish because she would read the Book of Mormon during the slow times. She would poke her pole out of the front hatch and lie in the cabin reading. So she could read and turn pages until a fish jerked her line, she would wrap the line around her toe.

Marie has always loved the Book of Mormon. In fact her younger brother, Lynn, claims that his love for the Book of Mormon came from Marie. Each day she would tell him what she had learned in her seminary class about it.

During Marie's earliest years, her father was in the military. Consequently, she spent part of her childhood living in Ford Hood, Texas, and Fort Sill, Oklahoma. When the family returned to Spanish Fork, she attended Rees Elementary School where she loved all of her teachers. Once when her sister, DeAnn, likened one of Marie's teachers to a sack of potatoes, Marie started to cry. The woman may have been plain in appearance, but Marie thought she was beautiful. Even at that young age, Marie's desire to be a teacher was beginning to germinate.

Blessed with a marked musical ability, Marie has been a singer since early childhood. She and a friend would often practice songs, in harmony, as they played on the swings in the backyard. Later, the two sang show tunes in local programs. And as a Spanish Fork High-School student, Marie sang in the a cappella choir and participated in the musical *The Music Man*. To this day, Marie can be heard humming the hymns or songs she has performed.

At an early age, Marie also learned that work can bring as much joy and satisfaction as play. She has fond memories of the many hours spent working in the yard with her family and recalls, with a smile, all that had to be done before she could go off to play. She still makes sure the lawn is mowed and the garden free of weeds before joining friends for a game of golf or tennis. If a fence needs painting or a car needs washing, the movie can wait—Marie works for fun.

All her early years of hard work, schooling, music, and recreation prepared Marie for her first teaching assignment. In 1969, when Marie signed a contract to teach third grade for Clark County School District in Las Vegas, Nevada, she began a five-year experience that would prove her competence. With her characteristic industry, Marie not only taught, but served as the supervisor of her school's reading lab and was the building coordinator for a continuous reading program. In 1971 and 1972, the Mt. View Elementary School recognized her with their Outstanding Teacher Award.

Marie loved teaching elementary school, but the desire to further her own education pulled her back to the university. In 1975, she returned to BYU to pursue a master's degree. But before completing her degree in August 1976, Marie's career took a new turn when she was hired by the Department of Elementary Education as a faculty member to work with students in their field experiences, including supervising student teachers. She also became BYU's most prominent teacher of reading and language-arts methods. The word on campus was "Tuttle's hard, but she's good!" For eleven years she was part of a four-member team that taught students in cohort groups. The students would begin with introductory education classes, work through basic methods courses, and end with student teaching.

In addition to her work at BYU, Marie has taught at BYU–Hawaii and Texas A&M University, where she received her doctorate in curriculum methods. The decision to pursue her doctorate was a natural one, and as she made plans to leave her family, friends, and BYU, the words of her Grandma Adamson once again helped her through. Marie often said of the experience, "It's not like I'm going out to fight the Indians." She completed her Ph.D. in December, 1995.

Truly a master teacher, Marie motivates and inspires her students, who consistently rate her as "exceptional" in their evaluations. Perhaps her greatest gift is the ability to effectively model the teaching skills she teaches. And she brings to her teaching a delightful sense of humor and a personality that has been called "terminally optimistic." Her motto: "Make Your Own Sunshine." Recognition for her zeal and competence came in 1985 when she was honored by the BYU Alumni Association and the graduating seniors in the Department of Elementary Education as Most Outstanding Teacher.

However, Marie's own greatest reward comes not so much from the honors and accolades, but from helping and watching her students progress. She frequently takes time to write letters of recommendation for students and, when they graduate, she invites them to keep in touch with her. Many send her wedding and birth announcements and notice of other special occasions. Some who have remained in the field interact with her now as friends and colleagues. She plays tennis with one of her former students and occasionally enjoys lunch and "teacher talk" with a number of others.

Marie concedes that teaching is more difficult now than it was twenty-five years ago. She feels that children today are unfortunately less respectful and at times "tougher." Children used to look up to a teacher with awe, while some children today are no longer even afraid of law-enforcement officers, let alone a teacher. She attributes this situation to more stress in the home and less supervision from the parents. To reach these children requires more skill. It also helps to have a good sense of humor. Marie believes that many a discipline problem in the classroom can be softened and sometimes resolved by a healthy dose of humor.

Although her schedule may be a busy one, Marie loves spending any spare time she has with her nephews—Matt, Jeff, Mark, and Brad—and niece, Shannon. The boys and their friends enjoy sleepovers at Aunt Marie's, so she sometimes goes to bed later than she had planned while four to eight pizza-filled boys sleep in her basement.

Marie's heart and soul have not only opened and stretched her own world, but also that of the relatives, friends, students, and associates who have been motivated by her example. She is an inspiration to all she meets to do something a little better, give a troubling situation one more try, smile, and see the lighter side of things.

Marion Bennion Stevens

College of Family, Home and Social Sciences

by

Erma Bennion Rollins and Marjorie Wight

Marion Bennion Stevens knew her subject matter well, both in theory and practice. If she were teaching students to make bread, she could demonstrate it with a superior loaf. If the subject were complex protein molecules, she had the ability to make the information seem simple. Marion served faithfully at Brigham Young University for twenty-seven years.

*T*he group at the missionary get-together sat entranced as beautiful music wafted from the piano. The pianist was enjoying herself. She turned to the group, smiled, and then turned back to the instrument, this time crossing her hands as she played with the same expertise and verve. Everyone clapped heartily, crowded around her, and joined in as she played songs they all knew. The missionary-pianist was Marion Bennion, and the setting was 1950 in the Kentucky-Tennessee Mission of the Church. Marion was the personal secretary in the mission home and when, in 1952, she was released, it was with glowing reports of her diligence and service.

Marion's proficiency on the piano goes back to her early life on the farm where she went one hour each day to a neighbor's piano to practice. The music was a release from the harshness of farm life. After the family obtained a piano she intensified her practice. Often at noon, when her father came in for his meal, he would get up from the table and ask her to play. She would do so while he would stretch out on the couch and listen. His favorite piece was "Kitten on the Keys," and Marion's favorite hymn was "I'm a Pilgrim."

When the first area conference of the Church was held at the University of Texas, El Paso, with President Ezra Taft Benson presiding, Marion Bennion Stevens was the organist for the entire conference. This, for her, was a highlight. She did not dream of such an opportunity when she grew up on a two-hundred-acre farm in Delta, Utah.

Marion's life began September 23, 1925, in Murray, Utah. She was the second child born to Sterling and Beryl Hamilton Bennion and was reared with her older brother, Sterling, and two younger sisters, Erma and Lucille. The family moved to the outskirts of Delta to a farm. It was difficult to make much financial gain there, but they worked hard and produced their own vegetables, meat, and dairy products. On any farm there is much to do and always a need for more farmhands. Occasionally Marion was called upon to tromp hay, but she had a strong preference for working in the house where her skills at cooking and sewing served her well—her homemade rolls were mouth watering, and she made most of her own clothes, a skill that later produced tailor-made suits.

Her education and career were thorough and successful—she continually excelled. In 1943, Marion graduated from Delta High School, after which she attended the Branch Agricultural College (now Southern Utah State University) in Cedar City, Utah, graduating in 1945. She then attended Brigham Young University for summer school—in order to work and study piano—and later went to Utah State University to pursue her chosen academic field, dietetics. In this choice Marion was inspired by her mother who had taught general home economics in high school.

At Utah State, Marion was inducted into Phi Kappa Phi (because of her outstanding academic record), into Omicron Nu (a professional society for home economists), and into an honorary student music society. She graduated from Utah State in 1947 with a B. S. degree in dietetics and became a licensed dietician after completion of an internship at the Columbia-Presbyterian Medical Center in New York City in 1948. During this time she was also enrolled as a graduate student at Teachers College, Columbia University. She then accepted a position as a therapeutic dietician in the medical wards of Presbyterian Hospital and continued taking evening classes at Columbia until she completed an M.A. degree in dietetics in 1949.

The following year took Marion to Idaho State College, where she accepted a position as instructor of foods and nutrition. It was then, after one year of teaching, that she accepted her mission call from the Church, came to serve as the mission president's secretary, and amazed her fellow missionaries with her piano antics.

Marion's career in the Department of Food Science and Nutrition at BYU began after her mission was completed in 1952. During her twenty-seven years at the university, she advanced from instructor to full professor, with responsibilities ranging from teaching to research, administration, university service, and professional service. She made a significant contribution in each of these areas. As a teacher at BYU, Marion not only became a role model, but a lifetime friend to many students who have distinguished themselves in the field of food science and nutrition. For her teaching excellence she was given the Karl G. Maeser Distinguished Teaching Award.

One of her students, Geneve Johns, has been a chief dietician at the University of Utah Hospital for many years. Geneve says of her training under Marion:

> When I left BYU, I interned at La Jolla Hospital in California. I was mingling with dietetic interns from all over the country. Some of them did not feel well prepared for the assignments we were given. I, on the other hand, had been taught all the basics and was well equipped for my internship. Marion's gift of confidence and knowledge has remained with me during my many years as a dietician.

Marion conducted research at BYU while teaching a heavy load, directing a medical dietetics program, and serving as department chair. She has published two advanced technical books, *The Science of Food* and *Clinical Nutrition*, which are fundamental works in her profession, as well as a much-used basic college text, *Introductory Foods*. As a result of her outstanding scientific research career, the BYU chapter selected her to give the Sigma Xi annual lecture in 1968.

Marion served as chair of the Food Science and Nutrition Department for twelve years. During this time the department became a strong academic unit and received great respect throughout the university, especially from faculty in the biological, physical, and health science areas. From 1973 to 1976, Marion served as director of the undergraduate program in medical dietetics and helped establish internships in hospitals along the Wasatch Front, so that her students could train to become registered dieticians. She spent countless hours traveling throughout the United States, helping to establish high-quality dietetics programs, and, in 1969, became a delegate to the White House Conference on Food, Nutrition, and Health. In 1992, she received the Utah Dietetic Association Award of Merit.

When Marion Bennion left the BYU Food Science and Nutrition Department, it was a department of superior rating. The challenge has been to keep it that way. Fortunately, other well-trained professors have maintained its high academic level. Ninety-five percent of the department's students pass the difficult national registered dietician exam successfully.

In 1977, Marion married Wayne Stevens, a rancher and chemical engineer. Marian Jensen, a colleague for a short while, remembers how Marion Bennion's gentle personality became more animated when she met and was courted by Wayne. Their marriage has been one of good companionship and professional productivity and collaboration. The couple lives in El Paso, Texas, where Marion is active in the local El Paso Dietetic Association, fills assignments for the American Dietetic Association, and until the last few years, has been a consultant and teacher at the El Paso Community College.

Even in her retirement, Marion continues to work consistently. Since 1982, she and her husband have been working on the development of a process to extract masoprocol from the Larrea plant (chaparral or creosote bush) that grows throughout the Southwest and Mexico. Masoprocol is a part of the final product called Actinex, which is being marketed by Block Drug Company. It is a product that is used in the treatment of some kinds of cancer.

Along with her professional pursuits, Marion has been involved in many activities in the LDS Church. She has been a teacher in Primary and the Young Women program, president of the El Paso Stake Relief Society, and has served many times as ward or stake organist. While she was teaching full time at BYU, she also acted as counselor to Alice Wilkinson in the first BYU young women's Relief Society.

Periodically, Marion reviews and updates her textbooks which are still in demand throughout the country. Included in some of these texts are pictures of teenagers licking ice cream cones or eating something nutritious. The teenagers are her own nephews and nieces, to whom she has always given special attention. One nephew, Alan Rollins, has received regular correspondences from his Aunt Marion and a niece, Lujean Anderson, has received some special family heirlooms. Marion's influence on her family members has been tremendous. She always made her parents proud of her and was a great support to them. As a token of respect for her mother, who motivated her career in food science, Marion established an endowed scholarship fund at BYU in 1975, the Beryl Hamilton Scholarship Fund, to which she still contributes. It gives scholarships each year to students in food science and nutrition. This unselfish act is a monument to her love of family, Brigham Young University, and her profession.

Ruth Elizabeth Brasher

College of Family, Home and Social Sciences

by

Carol Ellsworth,
Helen Brasher Mortensen, and Marjorie Wight

Dr. Ruth Brasher and others in the BYU Family Science Department are preparing people for family life—just as important an occupation as any professional endeavor. At one time, the Home Economics Division, for which Dr. Brasher has served as the head, had over five hundred students as majors. Now, because so many women are going into other fields, the number has dropped. But this division still boasts about 150 students—one of the largest home economics programs in the country.

*L*ights flash! A siren blares as the red fire truck speeds down the road toward the house on fire. The truck is parked; the firemen jump out and in one motion do what firemen do. "A child is still in there," a bystander yells, and with no hesitation several firemen race inside. All the watchers stand tense, hardly breathing. Then a cheer goes up. Carrying a person each, three firemen come out of the burning house. One of the rescued is a small girl, crying hysterically. The fireman holding her brings a colorful teddy bear from the truck and puts it in the little girl's arms. For a moment she looks at it, and then with a faint smile cuddles the teddy bear to her. Her crying stops.

This rather melodramatic scenario is, in fact, a reality in many emergencies in the Provo, Utah, area. How did it all come about? It began when leaders of the Provo Pleasant View Ninth Ward were deciding what project they could do to commemorate the 150th anniversary of the beginning of Relief Society. The subject of children in emergency crises came up, and Ruth Brasher told of the positive effect teddy bears can have at such times. The teddy-bear project was born, with Ruth as the inventor and chief production manager.

The project began with a commitment to provide the emergency fire department of Provo, Utah, with three hundred teddy bears. It has now grown far beyond that goal to almost three thousand teddy bears, delivered to various police departments, the local Children's Justice Center, emergency medical units, and "pink ladies" at hospitals. In June 1994 seventy bears were shipped to Russia. And eighty-five bears have already been sent to Kenya and Ghana.

The following excerpts from a news article tell of the effectiveness of the project:

Officer Bruce Wilkins, Orem Police Department, said that one small boy he was questioning was too emotionally upset to talk without crying. Wilkins gave him one of the teddy bears and the boy grabbed it, hugged it, and stopped crying. . . .

Donna Crawley of the Children's Justice Center said one child interviewed there picked out a pink bear and later told her mother that pink was her favorite color. . . .

Other officers and representatives of the Division of Family Services related how the children often take the bears to court with them and hug them while they are testifying. . . .

Another mother related that in the recuperation process of her young child from a traffic accident, she didn't know what had been the most effective for the child—the bear or the medication. . . ."

This original project, chaired by Ruth Brasher, has expanded greatly to other teddy-bear projects which are now going on in Florida and Illinois. Ruth was asked how long the project would continue and she answered, "Only as long as there are children."

—The Daily Herald, April 17, 1994

This tremendously successful project is proof of Ruth Brasher's administrative ability, as well as her concern for the needs of both little children and Relief Society women. The women make these bears from scraps of material from their homes and trim them with ribbon, lace, and other decorations.

Ruth Brasher's industry and competence reach far back into her childhood. She was born in Huntington, Utah, on September 3, 1929, in a home located on a dairy ranch operated by her father. She was the eldest of six children—five daughters and one son—born to Erma Elizabeth and Kenneth John Brasher.

Ruth grew up working in the home and, in many ways, became a second mother to her younger sisters and brother. But a dairy ranch requires many workers, so as Ruth matured, she helped out. During World War II, Ruth's summer job was to drive the dairy truck, delivering milk to the neighborhood towns. As she traveled many miles through Carbon and Emery Counties, she made the work pleasurable by listening to baseball games on the radio. She cheered for the New York Yankees and the Brooklyn Dodgers—but mostly for the Detroit Tigers. And of course the World Series was always a favorite event with Ruth. Even now, when she attends professional meetings throughout the country, she occasionally attends a baseball game.

Ruth received her childhood education in Emery County, Utah. After graduation from high school she attended the College of Eastern Utah, later transferring to Brigham Young University where she earned a B.S. in home economics education. Upon receiving a national 4-H fellowship, she selected the University of Maryland for her master's degree in adult education. In 1969 she completed her Ph.D. in sociology at Utah State University.

Dr. Brasher, who was actively involved in 4-H programs during her school years, chose to begin her professional life as a home economist with the Cooperative Extension Service in Carbon County, Utah. Later, she spent six months in the Philippines on the International Farm Youth Exchange program, where she lived and worked with farm families. Her career then took her to Utah County and later to Oregon as a 4-H specialist. In 1969, she returned to Brigham Young University's Family Science Department and began teaching and serving as chair of the Home Economics Division.

When Ruth teaches, she prepares thoroughly and imparts practical information that will make her students better homemakers. She has always tried to cooperate with the students and help them set their own goals. One semester some of her senior students in a curriculum and methods class were working on a project. The students wrote some curriculum that required Dr. Brasher to come to class one day in jeans. Ruth was no stranger to jeans—she had worn them frequently when she delivered milk from her dairy farm—but when she has taught at BYU, her appearance has always been that of a professional. So for Ruth, this request was somewhat difficult to fulfill. Yet she was determined to cooperate with her students. At home, she donned some jeans, pulled a skirt over them, and came to school. Then just before class, she removed her skirt and mingled with her students in her more casual attire. Her students appreciated her good sportsmanship.

Ruth remained in her position as division chair until she became associate dean of the College of Family, Home, and Social Sciences in 1980. Later, in 1989, she returned to full-time teaching. More recently she was appointed director of the Honor Code Office where she has worked with students who need strong leadership and help.

Since Ruth first came to BYU, she has served on dozens of committees, both as a member and as chair. One of her committee assignments was to co-chair the fund-raising for the development of the Camilla Eyring Kimball Chair of Home and Family Life. To accomplish this goal, she was given the job of raising one million dollars! Some of her colleagues expressed doubt that she would be able to do it, but she proved them wrong. We see in this example one of Ruth's most prized traits: when she decides to accomplish a goal, she pursues it until it is reached.

Ruth also helped establish the Camilla Eyring Kimball annual scholarship, which is given each year to a student to assist him or her in school expenses. Additionally, Dr. Brasher became coordinator for the development of the Endowment of the Virginia F. Cutler Faculty Lecture, which is delivered annually by an outstanding faculty member within the College of Family Living. One year, she herself was selected to give the lecture. Among Ruth's other numerous honors is also the Karl G. Maeser Outstanding Teaching Award.

Just as energetic in her Church assignments, Ruth served in the Central States Mission and in many other capacities, including two callings as stake Relief Society president—of the BYU Fifth and Tenth Stakes. For a period of time, Ruth was also a member of the Relief Society curriculum writing committee. She and her committee members wrote the lessons for the Social Relations and Home Management lessons in the Relief Society manuals during President Barbara Smith's tenure.

Her comment about being called as the Tenth Stake Relief Society president after serving in the Fifth Stake was, "I guess the Lord is giving me another chance to do the job right." However, there has never been any doubt that Ruth always "did the job right." More recently she has taught the Gospel Doctrine class in her Pleasant View Ninth Ward, and she enjoys singing soprano in the ward choir.

During these busy professional years, Ruth has been a source of strength and encouragement to her family. Helen Mortensen, Ruth's younger sister and the mother of six adopted children, attests to the fact that Ruth has played the role of a grandmother to her children. She has encouraged them to do well in school and, on occasion, has helped them financially. Careful to share special moments with them,

Ruth never forgets a birthday, a concert, a recital, or other event. She helps the children set and achieve specific goals·and may share a weekend with them—helping them read, playing games with them, and taking them on long walks.

Ruth Brasher always expects excellence in herself and the people with whom she works—but always in a way that motivates them to work to their potential. The introductory remarks at the Virginia F. Cutler lecture she gave to the College of Family Living refer to her many abilities and the popularity she has with others: "Dr. Brasher should be cloned. Then we would have a Ruth Brasher, full-time teacher, and a Ruth Brasher, full-time administrator." Ruth's dedication, hard work, and versatility are hallmarks of any position she holds or task she accepts. She has indeed made a significant contribution to her family, to her Relief Society associates, and to the students and faculty at Brigham Young University.

Lucille Nelson Jensen
College of Family, Home and Social Sciences

by

*Mary Louise Seamons,
Nicole Jensen Lyon, and Marjorie Wight*

"Miss Lucy"—loved by children, parents, college students, and faculty members alike—was the supervising teacher of the Brigham Young University Preschool Laboratory for many years. Mary Louise Seamons, a long-time colleague and friend, has written the following sketch, to which Lucille Jensen's daughter, Nicole, has provided valuable additions.

*L*ittle David, with a pack on his back, enters the classroom smiling and sits down. From his pack he takes out a green rubber dinosaur, a Tyrannosaurus Rex, and hands it to "Miss Lucy." She shows it to the class and an animated discussion ensues. Davie has brought "show and tell" items before: a special rock and a shell. He says he likes school because he has friends there—Blake and Charlie. But most of all he loves Miss Lucy because he knows she loves him.

Perhaps Miss Lucy relates so well to her preschool children because of memories from her own childhood—even glimmers from her infancy. When little Lucy Nelson was only three months old, her father, Obed Nelson, was called to serve on a short six-month mission to Denver, Colorado. Her mother, Tina Nelson, was a co-partner in this mission, caring for their four children during her husband's absence. Lucy claims to have a distinct remembrance of her father's return from this mission and the family's elation as they greeted him. When her father entered the kitchen, he lifted Lucy from her highchair and held her close. Lucy seems to remember that moment.

Lucy grew up in Mount Pleasant, Utah. Born on April 9, 1928, she was blessed with the name of Lucille. Though her mother did not believe in nicknames, her father always affectionately called her Lucy. She grew up with twin brother and sister, Leslie Ferdinand and Mary, and one more sister, Beverly.

Lucy's instinctive love for babies and toddlers was manifest early. As a schoolgirl she enjoyed caring for her friends' baby brothers or sisters, often while the friends went out to play. Loving this responsibility, Lucy would play with the babies until they were tired and then put them to sleep with her singing.

At Hamilton Elementary School she was active, friendly, and full of fun—qualities she has never outgrown. Frequently she participated in the grammar-school operettas. And while attending North Sanpete High School, she was involved in many extracurricular activities: the pep and service club, the commercial club, the school chorus, a play, and the publication of the yearbook.

Lucy and her friends, Lola Drage and Donna Lou Erickson, formed a vocal trio, which entertained at school, church, and community activities. At one time they were encouraged to cut a record and go professional. They were told they were better than the then-popular Andrews Sisters were when they got started. But a musical career for this local trio was not to be.

After graduating from North Sanpete in 1946, Lucy attended the University of Utah, graduating with a bachelor's degree in home economics. Her first teaching positions were in Vernal, Payson, and Logan, Utah.

In the mid 1950s Lucy started a master's degree in early childhood education at Kansas State University. One Christmas during this period, Lucy returned home to Utah for the holidays. There she renewed an old friendship with Kent Jensen from Fairview, Utah, who had just returned from four years in the Korean War. Things happened fast and the couple was married. They spent the rest of the holidays together, but at the end of the season, the new Mrs. Jensen returned to Kansas State to complete her degree, and her husband, Kent, returned to BYU.

After Lucy graduated from Kansas State, she and Kent settled in Provo. She was immediately hired by Dr. Blaine Porter to work in the newly organized College of Family Living. In 1956, she and Frances Barlow became the head teachers for the BYU Preschool and taught basic child-development classes to the university students.

The BYU Laboratory in Early Childhood Education is *not* a day-care center where mothers drop their children off for a full day. It provides a planned two-and-one-half-hour morning or afternoon session designed to enrich and brighten the day of a three- or four-year-old and prepare him for regular school. Parents also participate in the program; "Miss Lucy" schedules regular conferences with them about the progress of their children.

This program has expanded rapidly since its beginnings. The wonderful facilities plus the well-trained teachers make it unsurpassed—hence the long waiting list of children wanting to attend. As of 1995, fifty children, in two classes, attended every morning. For some time, BYU was the only university in the state with this early-childhood program. Thus, many potential kindergarten teachers throughout the state would enroll at BYU for the primary purpose of getting this specialized training and credential.

Music, arts and crafts, physical fitness, and reading readiness form the children's curriculum. Miss Lucy and her teaching assistants have weekly and daily planning sessions to ensure that each activity has a purpose. Every day includes a "free choice" period, a group musical or reading experience, a snack, a time for crafts (with finger paints or magic glue), and an outdoor period where the children can build sand castles or play on slides and tricycles.

The literature of early childhood has its own set of classics. *The Carrot Seed* by Ruth Kraus, for example, is one that the children ask to have read over and over again. ("Carrots grow from carrot seeds. I planted them. I'll water them. I'll pull the weeds. So my carrots soon will grow.") Another more current book, *Chika Chika Boom-Boom* by Bill Martin, is also a favorite. The children delight in trying to repeat its rhymes. ("A told B and B told C. I'll meet you at the top of the coconut tree. Whee, said D, to EFG, I'll beat you to the top of the coconut tree. . . . Chicka Chicka, Boom, Boom. Will there be enough room for us at the top of the coconut tree?") Lucy smiles as she reads these books to the children, or as she sings with them about the turtle called "Tiny Tim."

Snack time brings a fruit drink and a cracker. Lucy and the other teachers sit with the children and, by example, teach the children table manners. She remembers with fondness the day when one young child said to her, "Thank you for passing the crackers to us, so we won't grab." Sometimes the children are introduced to new foods, which they may not have ever tried. They learn to pour juice from a small pitcher, and if they spill, they clean it up with a special cloth. Once a year the children help make ice cream or butter.

In the summer, one day is devoted to outdoor activities. Miss Lucy and associates take the children outside where they can slide down the watered slide in their bathing suits, blow colored bubbles, paint the outside of the school with paint brushes dipped in water, and pour water in the sand pile to build whatever suits their fancy. Sometimes they wash their dolls with water and real soap and dry them clean. How children love water play!

If a squabble arises, the skilled veteran, Miss Lucy, is able to gently dissipate the angry feelings so enemies become friends within a matter of minutes. Lucy is wise enough to know that quarrelers can frequently solve their own differences without adult interference. She recalls one such quarrel in the sandbox between Eric and Jamie. Eric started throwing sand on Jamie, and Jamie became very upset. He said to Eric,

"If you do that again you'll go to the Devil."

Eric replied, "What's the Devil?"

"The Devil is a little red man who lives under the ground."

"How long will I have to stay with him?"

"You'll have to stay there two days, three hours, and forty-five seconds."

This straightforward reply put a stop to Eric's sand-throwing, and the boys resumed their building. Lucy, listening nearby, had let them work out their own differences.

On the home front, Lucy has always had the same quiet competence with her own children. She and Kent are the parents of four children: Michael, Jeffrey, Nicole, and Jennifer. Nicole remembers her mother as patient, calm, and supportive. She also remembers the lullabies she would sing to the children when they were ready for sleep. And in the kitchen, Lucille is unforgettable: lasagna, casseroles, chocolate pies, and fruit sherbet, made with the fruits of the season. Nicole remembers many a cookie-baking session with her mother.

All that good cooking made Lucy's youngest son, Jeff, especially happy. Active in athletics, this tall, young man (now married) had an enormous appetite. What a job, keeping that stomach satisfied! Attending Jeff's football games was a favorite family activity.

The Jensens loved the holidays and would frequently light a fire in the fireplace. As they would assemble around it, an unofficial member of the family, Danny (a Highland Scottie), would seat himself directly in front of the fire to feel the heat. How they all laughed!

Of course, no family is without challenges. During adolescence, one of Kent and Lucy's children was afflicted with a serious illness. They were devastated when they learned that no cure for the illness had been discovered. Though their son has still not been "cured," he has made progress. The Jensen's have remained strong through it all, and they are grateful their son is now independent.

For a few years Lucy left the BYU Preschool to live in Salt Lake, so her husband, Kent, would be closer to his business. His clothing store, the Brownstone, expanded, and he soon established other quality men's stores in Ogden, Utah, and in Arizona. Finally, about fifteen years ago, BYU prevailed on Lucille Jensen to return to their early childhood program. Her own children were fairly well established by this time, so she accepted the offer. For a few years she commuted from her Holladay home to Provo. When that became difficult, Lucy and Kent made the decision to return their residence to Provo. Lucy could get to work in ten minutes, and Kent now took his turn at commuting to Salt Lake.

In September 1991, Lucy was appointed to an administrative position in her department. She now had complete responsibility over the preschool. A conscientious worker, Lucy could often be seen preparing lessons during early morning hours, lunch periods, and evenings. Perhaps she would also make more play dough, mix poster paints, or set up the snack tray.

As one would expect, Lucy's abilities with children have been a great asset to the Church. She has served a fifteen-year stint in the Primary, in addition to her work in various other organizations. And as a grandmother, she guarantees that four grandchildren receive plenty of special attention, even transporting them long distances to dance or music lessons.

Lucy has certainly been well loved by faculty, students, parents, and children. One former preschooler, now grown up, was working part time as a BYU student custodian in the preschool. One day as he cleaned and rearranged the tables and chairs, he spoke to one of the teachers: "You know, this is a part of my custodial work that is fun because of memories I have. When I was four years old I came to this preschool. I remember the school, but most of all I remember Miss Lucy. She was my favorite teacher."

After twenty years he still remembered her! And Lucy seemed to know how much the children have all loved her. One day Meredith, another preschooler, was trying to express her feelings for Miss Lucy: "I love you more than the whole world weighs!" The more mature words of a colleague express the same feelings:

Miss Lucy may well be the most loved employee on campus. Over the more than fifteen years she has served in the campus preschool, she has been loved by over a thousand children and the hundreds of BYU students who have worked with her. Lucy is an individual who works as skillfully with the shy child as with the hyperactive one, with the hesitant student as with the highly confident one, and also works well with a whole range of parental concerns. In all our years of association with Lucy, we have never once seen her lose patience with a child, student, parent, faculty member, or staff colleague.

Early in the 1993 school year, Lucille Jensen was in a serious automobile accident. Her car was totaled by another driver, and she experienced whiplash and back injuries. Following this accident, Lucy began to have severe headaches, which forced her to stay in bed for ten weeks. When she returned to the preschool, she found it difficult to get up and down with the children. This accident was perhaps the biggest factor leading to her retirement in the spring of 1994.

Her associates accepted her decision with regret. One colleague, Dr. Thomas Draper, stated at the time: "It will be the end of an era. Lucy's preschoolers, university students, colleagues, and the others whose lives she has touched will remember Miss Lucy far into the future."

Maxine Lewis Rowley

College of Family, Home and Social Sciences

compiled from interviews with

Mary Beth Christensen,
Jenefer Rowley, and Maxine Rowley

Maxine Rowley's amazingly thorough training in all the disciplines of home economics education—clothing and textiles, fashion merchandising, family relations, child development, curriculum writing, and research—are all part of what makes her the remarkable teacher she is. But the most important aspect of her teaching is her concern for her students.

*I*n 1994 Maxine Lewis Rowley received a telephone call informing her that the graduating seniors of Brigham Young University's Family Sciences Department had once again voted her their outstanding teacher. (It was the sixth time in a row!) The person making the call then asked if she could define what she did that had earned her the award so many times. Dr. Rowley replied, "I'm not sure. It's such a large department, and I foster the professional preparation of so few."

Those few have come to form a national network of professionals over the years who see Maxine Rowley as a progressive leader, mentor, and friend. One attorney, Robert Vail, wrote, "I never took a class from her; she advised me in an honorary. She was the person most responsible for my being a national officer and my acceptance to law school." A second young man, who later became a computer programmer, wrote to Maxine, "Your Family Science 300 course this semester has been most enjoyable. Most courses at BYU do not merit such applause, but I want to tell you that I have appreciated your class. Thank you for your service and flexibility with us, your students."

Just one indication of Maxine's thoroughness in teaching is that she teaches the crucial skill of writing in every one of her classes (her first college degree included an emphasis in magazine editing). Colleagues and friends who see the extraordinary amount of time she spends with both graduate and undergraduate students, and their research and writing, have sometimes cautioned her to spend her time more wisely. Upon her advancement to the rank of associate professor, one of her administrators sent a letter congratulating her, and then added, "We cannot fault your citizenship or your teaching ability and evaluations, and it is obvious that you can write. But you should write and publish more in prestigious journals." He had no way of knowing that much of the time she devotes to writing and editing secures first publications for former students working through graduate programs, often in departments located at other universities.

In fact, Maxine continues to mentor her students long into their professional careers, whether or not those careers are part of her own discipline. One of these professionals, whose present salary and position outrank Maxine's, has written, "She always focuses on people

over things, and I think she must count her own success in the accomplishments of others. I actually set aside in my monthly budget an
amount to pay for telephone calls to her. And she understands that
communication is much more than just talk."

Maxine's husband and children, who have watched her receive
honor after honor from her students, tease her about the fact that she
once decided she would never be three things: a wife, a mother, or a
teacher. Her journey in becoming and excelling in precisely these
three roles, and her selection of a field dedicated to families, parenting, and homemaking, say much about her underlying values and her
ability to adapt to changing circumstances.

Maxine Lewis Rowley was born September 23, 1938, in Provo,
Utah, to Max Thomas and Illa Hale Lewis. Her father was a cattle
rancher and part-time forest ranger who died at the age of thirty-nine,
leaving his wife, an artist and secretary, to raise four children. Maxine
was the second child and the oldest girl.

She had originally set her sights on becoming a medical doctor,
but her mother gave no support to her sixteen-year-old daughter's
wish to accept an early academic scholarship to Stanford University.
Instead Maxine accepted a scholarship to Brigham Young University
and started as a freshman there. She not only took a full academic
load, but also worked full time—her scholarship did not quite cover
all her expenses and her widowed mother needed help at home.

Her original career goals changed after a series of BYU advisors
and department chairs counseled her out of medicine and then chemical engineering, which were then considered "men's professions."
She also recalls that, finally, after being told by a member of the nursing faculty that she looked "too pale and skinny" to be a nurse, she
went to the library and researched careers that seemed to be focused
on the world of women. Since she liked to write, she elected a career
in fashion-magazine editing and graduated in 1960 with a B.A. in
clothing and textiles and journalism.

At this time, Maxine was told by an administrator that she had
been a strong contender for valedictorian, but it was felt the honor
should go to someone who "holds the priesthood." The trophy she

was given that spring was engraved "Outstanding Woman Student, Brigham Young University."

Following graduation, Maxine's goals continued to change. On her twenty-first birthday, she married Arthur William Rowley, a young convert to the church. He had recently returned home from serving in the armed forces, where he had helped establish one of the LDS branches in Germany and had even served as its first branch president.

For Maxine, the decision to marry resulted in several missed opportunities. Shortly before the wedding, a contract to be an editor for the new Church magazine, *The New Era*, was rescinded because the administrator in charge learned that she was engaged. That same year she turned down an offer for an editorship with *Mademoiselle* magazine. But Maxine was later able to replace these editorships with two other jobs: writing for KCPX radio and for the Utah State University Extension Service.

For the most part, Maxine devoted the next ten years to being a wife and the mother of two daughters. Then her husband, Arthur, had a serious accident in which both of his legs and other parts of his body were crushed. He had to undergo months of hospitalization, surgery, and rehabilitation, and because he was self-employed, his income came to a halt. Maxine was told repeatedly that her husband would probably not live.

The situation was complicated by the young ages of their children—Anne was five years old and Jenefer only three. Maxine was also responsible for the care of her mother, who was undergoing a series of bone surgeries, and the support of some Polynesian missionaries to whom the Rowleys had made commitments. She decided to work as a night-time reporter so that during the day she could function as the only nurse and housekeeper they could afford. Meanwhile, Arthur fought to live, then to become well enough to use a wheelchair, and finally, to walk again.

The Rowleys received help and blessings from a variety of sources: a couple across the street, Leora and Jay Spenberg, came to their rescue often; they ate from the family food storage; and they were blessed with a strong faith and determination that all would be well. The new family car was traded for a second-hand one that had to be pushed home from church every Sunday, but the family remained solvent and the missionaries remained in the field. By 1972, after Arthur could resume some work, Maxine had enrolled in a home-economics program at the University of Utah that would qualify her to teach school. She could see that teaching would allow her to keep the same hours as her children.

When she entered the University of Utah, Maxine's intent was to receive an M.A. and a teaching certificate, but the program was phased out before she completed it. So she obtained a second bachelor's degree, this time in home economics education. Yet even with this new focus, her first teaching job included classes that allowed her to build upon her earlier education in fashion and merchandising. She taught high school and junior high school and later became a school guidance counselor.

Balancing career and family is never easy, but Maxine has always tried to do her best, especially by fostering family traditions and values that make life worthwhile. When she was fourteen years old, she did some of her genealogy, so her children have grown up intimately acquainted with the lives of their ancestors. Maxine is also a believer in the importance of heroes and has especially sought out heroes— both men and women—who make good role models for young women. Her favorite heroine is Ellen H. Richards, the first woman to graduate from M.I.T. and the founder of the American Home Economics Association. And in keeping with her great enthusiasm for her country, Maxine's patriotic heroes include George Washington, Thomas Jefferson, and John Adams.

Patriotism is a way of life for Maxine. She once elected to leave a graduate-level class early in order to vote before the polls closed, even though the professor warned her that her grade would be cut if she did. Her children remember that she always found a flag-raising ceremony for them to attend on the Fourth of July. Sometimes the Rowleys were the only ones present.

Maxine's teaching salary was meager for a family of five, and she soon realized she would have to increase it through more education. She then earned an M.S. at Utah State University in home economics education, with an emphasis in parenting—a subject she felt was more important than some of the standard, somewhat "outdated" home-economics skills: "how to iron a shirt in six minutes," or "how to make cake batter with six-hundred stirs." She wanted something that was really important and applicable to herself and others.

With this new direction in place, Maxine also launched into a doctorate. In 1989, twenty years after she had obtained her first degree at BYU, Maxine earned her Ph.D. at that same institution. And by this time, she had served on the faculty at both USU and BYU.

On one occasion a colleague remarked that Maxine Rowley was the most liberated woman he knew, to which Maxine laughed and said, "If I were really liberated, I would have taken one of the offers I received to go out of state for at least one of my degrees." This comment and another one made to her students, that "trying to be both a mother and a career woman has made me less effective at each job," are two rare indications from her that things have sometimes been difficult.

Maxine Rowley is a vital link between the BYU Family Science Department and national and state secondary-school programs. She has served as a liaison between BYU and the Utah State Office of Education for more than a decade and has been on the certification teams for most of Utah's post-secondary institutions. She is recognized as a national consultant and has been repeatedly called on for assistance by state departments of education from California to New Hampshire.

Her numerous awards include the prestigious American Home Economics Association State and National Teacher of the Year Award, as well as their National Leader Award. Her students have established in her name the only Kappa Omicron Nu Endowment for a current teacher and advisor of this national honorary for professionals in family and consumer sciences.

Maxine's contributions to the home economics profession have been overwhelmingly received. At one time, she was asked to give an address before a large audience at a national American Home Economics convention. She received a standing ovation, and afterwards received a number of offers from other universities where her salary would have been substantially increased. She declined these offers because she felt it would not have been wise to leave Utah or her family.

Maxine has served on dozens of national committees and produced volumes of curricula. For almost two decades her free enterprise and career exploration curriculum guides have been mandated by schools in many states and in Europe. And because of her expertise, she was asked to contribute an article on "Home-based Industry" to the *Encyclopedia of Mormonism.*

With practical experience in every facet of home economics, Maxine has made ongoing contributions at the community level as well. For example, in 1977 Dr. Rowley was named *Family Circle* magazine's National Teacher of the Year, and in 1994 the American Cancer Society honored her for her volunteer service and guidance in the successful completion of their classic, longitudinal research projects linking cancer, nutrition, and tobacco. The latter award indicates that Maxine's academic interests are not much different today than they were in high school when she claimed that geometry and chemistry were her main interests. She admits, though, that her mother fostered two of her greatest loves—history and poetry—to the degree that her oldest daughter, Anne, has said that when her mother really wants to indulge herself, "it is usually to do something intensely patriotic or to read history or poetry."

Mary Beth Christensen, a former student and a home economics teacher at Ricks College, writes:

> Maxine's greatest contribution has been her work with the students. It is not uncommon for students to approach her after class, wait outside her office, or call her at home. She is a builder of student self-worth, she is intuitive, and she sees the "genius" in students and pulls it out. During one of her early years at BYU,

when she held the rank of instructor, her students nominated her for the Karl G. Maeser Teaching Award, an honor usually reserved for seasoned full-time professors.

Such rapport with her students often leads to Maxine's spending entire evenings returning telephone calls—to present and former students. She believes that once a student is accepted to BYU, each teacher and administrator has a moral obligation to help the student succeed. When a Church leader asked her once what she considered to be her greatest weakness as a teacher, she said, "I nurture my students." He smiled and asked, "What is your greatest strength?" She looked him straight in the eye and replied, "I nurture my students."

Maxine Rowley once thought she would not be a wife, mother, or teacher. What a fortunate twist that she became all three, and that, according to her youngest daughter Jenefer, her greatest teaching— whether it be in lectures, speeches, or articles—has to do with the home. Jenefer quotes her mother as saying that "home should be quiet, personal and private, with spaces to share and spaces to be alone; a place where I can be with my Prophets, my Poets, and my Patriots; a place where I can be at peace and be in love."

Olga Dotson Gardner
College of Fine Arts and Communications
by
Kristen Gardner Spears

Olga Gardner proves that a mother of eight can successfully com-bine motherhood with the development of a marvelous talent. Of course, her family, and especially her husband, provide her with encouragement. Olga's daughter, Kristen, says of her father, "When mother sings, my father watches and listens with a pride bordering on adoration. He has been her greatest supporter."

*P*erhaps it was fortuitous that Olga Dotson was born near the musical and show-business capital of the world. She was welcomed into Burbank, California, by her parents, A. Lewis Dotson and Lola Irene McAdams on March 13, 1924. She was their sixth child.

Early in her upbringing her doting family recognized that pretty Olga had a great gift for song and drama. An excerpt from her diary gives us a glimpse into her activities:

> My oldest brother, Paul, after suffering through four sisters in a row, had so hoped for a baby brother that he was gravely disappointed in me. He would have nothing to do with me at first. But before long, he was noticed taking little peeks at me, and we soon became best pals. He used to let me polish his white shoes before all his dates, and then he often took me to his dance-band jobs, where he played trombone and bass fiddle. I was allowed to sing with the band, even when I was very little. During those years, we lived near the Culver City Motion Picture Studios. My cousin with her long dark curls and I with my long blond ringlets used to sing duets and act together in the training program for silent films at the studio.

Olga performed throughout her childhood and had many good teachers who gave her opportunities to sing. In high school, she did housework to pay for lessons with Walter Welti, a voice teacher at Utah State University. When she was a junior, he gave her an opportunity to sing a small role in the opera *La Traviata*. The next summer, her family moved to Salt Lake City, Utah, primarily so she could study with Emma Lucy Gates Bowen, a retired opera singer of significant reputation. Olga darned socks, fixed lunches, ran errands, and dusted to pay for these lessons.

After great experiences her senior year with her choral director at East High School, Lisle Bradford, Olga was then given a scholarship to Utah State, where she worked again with Walter Welti. Just before she turned eighteen, she sang the lead opera role as Gilda in *Rigoletto* in downtown Logan's Capitol Theater. The next year, she soloed with Richard Condie in a production of *The Creation* by Haydn.

At the end of her sophomore year of college, in 1933, Olga traveled to Boston and married John Hale Gardner, her high-school sweetheart. There, while continuing her singing pursuits and studying at the Boston New England Conservatory, Olga became pregnant with her first child. Her school career ended, but her voice training and performances continued. In fact, her professional engagements helped the family survive financially while her husband obtained his Ph.D. at Harvard.

Olga returned to Utah in 1949 and began a new career, as a BYU faculty wife, when her husband joined the Physics Department. Fast becoming known in the Provo area for her singing, she sang in church, at funerals, weddings, and clubs. But in this environment, she was rarely paid for her services. From this point on she has given freely of her time and talents without financial compensation. She feels her talent is a gift from God.

Olga has, however, had the opportunity to continue in several professional capacities. She played the lead soprano role in numerous operas for the Utah Valley Opera Association and sang and soloed in the Tabernacle Choir for seven years. She has also taught voice lessons.

In a BYU workshop she once directed, she related an incident that shows her incredible determination as a singer and her energy for life. She had a leading role in a Christmas *Messiah* production. Her schedule before the event was particularly busy, especially with the hostessing of a student wedding reception at her home. As the date for the event approached, she noticed that her singing voice was going. Immediately she applied some familiar home remedies (lemon and warm water, and honey and warm water), but to no avail. Her voice had become almost whisper-like. True to Olga's sense of commitment, she was determined to fulfill her obligation. So her doctor, to the rescue, sprayed her throat with something powerful; her voice came back, and she performed magnificently.

Olga was eventually invited to teach voice lessons at BYU—even though she had not earned a degree—because of her fine reputation as a singer and teacher. During this period she directed several student recitals and also starred in the lead soprano role in a *Madame Butterfly* production. She was an active participant in BYU Women, Literary League, and NATS (National Association of Teachers of Singing).

Along with all of her professional involvements, Olga raised eight children, all of whom became musicians. Each selected an instrument and practiced and performed as part of his or her childhood experience. Olga hosted numerous affairs in her home in support of her husband's faculty and BYU branch-president responsibilities. Her children remember cleaning the house in preparation for these events—their reward for their efforts was being allowed to stay up for the interesting entertainment and conversation in the living room. Her son, John, writes the following tribute to Olga:

Ever since I was a teenager, I haven't been able to even think about my mother's singing without a few tears. She was truly a great mother, and always an example for her children of one who developed her talents fully, managed uncomplainingly all the household needs, and always displayed the love and concern for her children that only a mother can. She was there when we came home from school and was ready to take care of our cuts and bruises—both physical and emotional. And although she worked hard on her singing, her first priority was her children. I once heard of a famous pianist, who after giving a concert, had a woman come up to him and say, "Wow, I'd give half my life to be able to play like that." He responded with, "I gave all of mine." In a way, this is like my mother. Although she was always at home and available when we needed her, she was also always working—listening to opera, singing, or teaching voice students.

While I was a teenager, I remember mother singing in three operas (*La Boheme, La Traviata,* and *Il Trovatore* with Utah Valley Opera Association). I remember her having dinner ready, then leaving for rehearsals four or five nights a week during those months. I have never been able to figure out how she had so much energy to do all of this and manage our home and family as well. And through it all, she always boosted our self-image—she had unconditional love for each of us and made sure we knew it.

Over time Olga became such a popular voice teacher on campus that she had to put in long hours, both at home and school, so she could accommodate all the BYU students on her long waiting list. She has had many classical voice students, but because she was willing to learn new techniques like the "belt" method, she also became popular among the musical drama students. The "belt" method actually enabled her classical voice students to open up more and keep their voices healthy as well. Thus, Olga has added a new dimension to her teaching techniques over the years that has continued to keep her in demand as a teacher.

During her family and professional careers, Olga endured three back surgeries. Her children say she is still erect, but a trifle shorter—both the surgeries and the law of gravity seem to have had their way. Nevertheless, she still teaches voice three days a week and finds time to enjoy her husband's retirement and her family—growing now, with grandchildren and great-grandchildren. Since her husband, too, has had back surgery, the two are able to empathize with one another. Olga is still active with BYU Women, several women's clubs, singing engagements, and church activities. Recently she has directed an annual ward concert, recruiting all the talent from ward members. These concerts have been the ward "hit" productions of the year. She does indeed maintain her youthful vigor.

Rosalie Rebollo Pratt

College of Fine Arts and Communications

by

Elise Bair

Dr. Rosalie Pratt's enthusiasm for her work, which combines her love and gift for music with the fields of education and medical science, is impressive—even infectious. This profile, originally titled "When You Find Yourself Redirected," first appeared in the May 1994 issue of Latter-day Women Magazine and is reprinted here with permission from Grandin Book Company, Provo, Utah.

ifteen years ago, Mary was diagnosed with an inoperable astrocytoma in her spine and has been progressively losing physical sensation in her body. Most who suffer from this kind of tumor spend the remaining years of life in wheelchairs, unable to move any of their limbs. However, when Mary learned of her astrocytoma, rather than surrendering herself to this fate, she resolved to do everything she could to counteract the effects of the disease.

After searching many avenues for a remedy, Mary discovered that when she listened to a very steady rhythm she could imitate the beat through physical movement. Before this breakthrough, she had been rapidly losing her ability to pronate and supinate (rotate) her wrists. But when she listened to a metronome and yielded her body to the rhythm, she gained greater rein over her movements. Even when she increased the metronome's speed, she could keep up. The outside stimulant gave her the rhythmicity she had lost in her body.

A daily exercise routine, using very rhythmic music in place of the metronome, has kept Mary in shape since her astrocytoma developed. Today, despite having only five percent of the normal range of physical sensation, this amazing woman can walk, roller-skate, ride her bike, drive her car—all activities neurologists predicted she would have to give up fifteen years ago.

Mary is one example of the thousands of people who have discovered in music a remedy that has yet to be found in medication. Her story is a favorite of Rosalie Pratt, professor of music at Brigham Young University. Dr. Pratt teaches courses in the philosophy of music education, the history and sociology of music and education, the influence of music on behavior, and other courses related to music medicine.

Dr. Pratt is the faculty advisor for the BYU Hospital Arts Program, which provides an opportunity for students and community members to share vocal and instrumental music with hospital patients. Participants in this two-year-old program regularly visit patients at Utah Valley Regional Medical Center and at the forensic unit of the Utah State Mental Hospital. The program is very informal;

the performers walk through the wards, asking patients if they would like to hear a familiar hymn or song. Rehearsed numbers are occasionally interspersed among the spontaneous performances. "Sometimes," says Dr. Pratt, "we gather the patients in small groups in the dining area of the stroke unit and play their favorite songs, and they sing along with us. It's quite a heartwarming thing, especially if you can bring a little lightness and joy to someone who has been lying there all day and would like to hear a favorite song."

Dr. Pratt's interest in music as a healing force has deep roots in her past. In fact, her career as an educator and researcher was preceded by a very different career—that of a concert harpist.

A Promising First Career

Rosalie Pratt first became interested in the harp at age thirteen when her New Jersey choir director offered to provide harp lessons for her. Under this director's tutelage, Rosalie developed a love for the instrument. After practicing and performing throughout her early teenage years, she entered Manhattanville College at age sixteen, where she pursued more intensive study.

While attending Manhattanville, she was invited to perform at a Catholic diocesan event at the Westchester Country Club, where Francis Cardinal Spellman happened to be in attendance. Rosalie was astonished to receive a call from his office a few days later inviting her to study in Italy as one of only eleven students handpicked from the United States.

Rosalie moved to Florence in 1954, where she attended the Pius XII Institute of Fine Arts. She spent four hours each day practicing the harp and studied many facets of Italian art as well. She reflects, "I was very young and excited about the adventure of it. What was unique was that I was living in the most culture-laden country and city on the planet, surrounded by the greatest art in the world: the cathedrals, the paintings, the sculptures, wonderful schools of music, conservatories, and great musical events. It was incredible."

In addition to earning her master's degree during her three years in Florence, Rosalie married an Italian engineer and gave birth to the first of two daughters.

Soon after her formal professional debut in Florence at the Cherubini Conservatory, Rosalie began a long series of performances that established her as a premier harpist in Europe. Besides traveling and performing in many countries, she also played for the Italian Radio Corp.

Later, back in the United States, Rosalie embarked on her career as a concert harpist, playing as principal for the New Jersey Symphony Orchestra, and was featured by several other orchestras. Her solo performances at Avery Fisher Hall and Carnegie Hall were reviewed in the New York Times. It was during this same time that she married her second husband, Sam Pratt, and became a member of The Church of Jesus Christ of Latter-day Saints.

In the course of her career as a performer, Rosalie recorded two professional albums: *Folk Songs with Troubadour Harps* and *Rosalie Pratt—Harpist*. She played for many celebrities and dignitaries, including Jason Robards and Jacqueline Onassis. Performances at Carnegie Hall and on television complemented her professional resumé.

But just when her first career had taken root, the effects of a plaguing disease set in, and as time progressed Rosalie realized she would have to redirect her life's efforts.

First Signs of Illness

When she was thirty-six years old, Rosalie began losing the finger dexterity so necessary to her career. The culprit was diagnosed as scleroderma, which prompts hardening of the skin and loss of flexibility. A connective tissue disease, scleroderma is an autoimmune disorder, one of a category of diseases in which the immune system becomes overactive. In essence, the body turns against itself. In the case of scleroderma, the body produces calcium deposits and abnormal, glue-like collagens in the joints and the skin. Today, Rosalie's scleroderma has progressed to the point that she cannot straighten her fingers. When it first developed, she tried to keep playing, but her ability was constrained by her stiff fingers. Eventually, playing became so painful that it was useless to continue. Rosalie formally stopped playing in 1979.

Redirected

Losing the ability to freely play the harp devastated Rosalie. For quite some time, nothing compensated for the loss. During her harp career, however, she had begun teaching music in elementary schools. As time passed, Rosalie's background as an educator and her own impaired circumstances drew her to special education. Before ending her career as a harpist (and knowing the eventual, debilitating course her disease would take), she returned to school to earn a doctoral degree in music education at Columbia University.

After leaving the public schools, she taught harp and teacher education at the college level. She also directed the music education program at Montclair State College. Over time, she became well established in her second career—that of music medicine research and education.

Since shifting from her original career as a concert harpist, Dr. Pratt has devoted herself to the field of music medicine. Her enthusiasm for her studies and her interest in natural approaches to physical ailments are evident as she talks about the history of music medicine: "Music as therapy has existed since the early roots of civilization," she explains. "The ancient Greeks and Romans believed that music and medicine were very closely allied. Writings attributed to Hippocrates and Galen show the importance of music in the ancient Greek curriculum. Long before the development of formal music therapy programs, people recognized similarities between the pulse of the heart and the pulse of music.

"Throughout the Middle Ages, music was very much a part of the curriculum of all educated students. Whether you were going to become a lawyer or a doctor or whatever, it didn't really matter—you studied music first. Then we became very specialized, and we began drifting off into our little grave-plots of knowledge."

Dr. Pratt believes that the nonspecialized approach gave people a holistic view of changes in body conditions. "Many doctors," she contends, "have lost the idea of looking at the whole person. An ailment may be manifest in a patient's throat. But what about her whole being? And what does her background and her thinking have to do with her health?" She continues, "I think that too much of the Western approach to medicine has relied on looking at symptoms alone and not looking beyond that." Dr. Pratt emphasizes that an understanding of the creative arts and medicine helps the physician in designing a treatment for the whole being, not just a single symptom.

While she is not a music therapist herself, music therapy is one aspect of her work as a scholar in music medicine. Music therapy became fully organized in the 1950s with the founding of the National Association for Music Therapy. This was followed in the 1970s by the organization of the American Association for Music Therapy. (Both organizations grant registration or certification to people who have fulfilled certain requirements in approved coursework and programs.)

From these efforts came the broader field of music medicine, which encompasses not only therapy but research, clinical practice, and the theory of music's influence on human physiology and psychology.

Current Projects

Dr. Pratt has recently assisted graduate student Jill Peterson Lex with her master's thesis: "The Effects of Biofeedback Training and Selected Music Interventions on Cardiac Chronotropic Control of Women in Childbirth." This project followed expectant mothers through their pregnancies and involved six music sessions administered to two groups of women. Each participant listened to her own musical selections. "They chose from a wide variety. We offered them all kinds of things: new age, classical, anything they wanted. A lot of them liked George Winston or Enya; some preferred Chopin. It's a very individual thing."

The control group focused only on music listening, but the second group was also instructed in biofeedback skills and relaxation techniques such as abdominal breathing and stress reduction through visualization. At the onset of her labor, each woman would alert Jill, who then provided her with the same music she had listened to in the six training sessions. At the hospital, the music was furnished through a special stereo that fits inside a pillow, allowing the woman to listen without having to use headphones. Dr. Pratt and Jill would then monitor her heart rhythmicity at various intervals (at dilation of four, five, and six centimeters) by means of a portable EKG (electrocardiogram) to observe her body's response. They found that the overall heart rate was lower and heart rate variability was increased for women in the biofeedback group. In addition, women who had participated in the biofeedback sessions were less likely to request epidurals or heavy medications than were women in the control group.

Dr. Pratt summarizes these results by saying. "Women in a stress-reducing mode are less likely to be panicked about the birth, and therefore their babies may have a less traumatic experience; everybody wins. Music and biofeedback training appear to evoke parasympathetic system responses, which translates into a calmer state for the mother."

This study, in particular, illustrates why music medicine appeals so strongly to Dr. Pratt. She emphasizes that using music does not interfere with natural processes. "It is not interfering with the woman or baby in any way that could be even slightly construed as invasive."

Another of Dr. Pratt's research projects, working with young boys diagnosed with Attention Deficit Disorder (ADD), also embraces the theme of noninvasive therapy. Perhaps she has even more at stake personally with these studies than with the childbirth studies; two of her grandsons have the disorder. ADD affects more males than females and does not appear to be a respecter of age or background. Symptomatic of this disorder, children with ADD do not operate on a task-behavior level. When an ADD child is on task, the brain waves, rather than activating a 13–21 hertz range (the frequency of beta waves), stay at 4–7 hertz (the frequency of theta waves). This lower level is typical of the daydreaming state. Affected children do not focus as other people do. As a result, many—from parents to teachers—view these children as disobedient, impulsive, and difficult to work with. Peer groups see them as social outcasts. They don't seem to be able to play sports well and are often avoided because of their impulsiveness and unsocial behavior.

Dr. Pratt is currently working with sixteen boys on a simple program to encourage them to concentrate. She has each boy sit in front of a computer and work with a system that encourages concentration. When he concentrates enough, he activates his beta range and his reward is the sounding of a beep. An exercise as uncomplicated as this builds his sense of achievement and encourages him to think on a more focused plane than he has before. More complex exercises use computer programs that reward a child for concentrating.

"I start with easy reward levels and gradually make the task a little bit harder and a little bit harder, so that earning rewards becomes gradually more difficult. I'm pushing him and pushing him a little at a time, until I finally get him into the beta range." Getting a consistent beta reaction takes at least forty practice sessions, but once a child with ADD can reach beta-level thinking, it positively affects other crucial areas of his life.

About her older grandson with ADD, Dr. Pratt says, "We found that when he had this training he suddenly went from a social outcast to having a lot of friends. He improved in sports, began attending class, and learned to follow directions. He was learning to 'stay with it.'" This simple training can influence ADD-affected children so greatly that teachers and peers begin to see the child as a whole new person. It is often important to give children regular booster sessions to maintain the improvements of the initial intensive-training period.

Dr. Pratt is quick to point out that this "new child" is actually a manifestation of the child's real personality that had previously been blocked by the ADD. This transformation is not the same one that occurs when the child is given large doses of a medication like Ritalin, which can suppress objectionable behaviors in affected children. About these drugs, Dr. Pratt says, "Although medication may often help, isn't it better to try a noninvasive approach first? You may suppress the behavior, but if you're not addressing the real problem, you're covering it up. Sooner or later, you've got to come back and address the problem."

She is especially concerned that the long-term effects of these strong drugs are not yet known. Side effects such as stunted growth, hallucinations, and involuntary muscle movement have been reported. Conversely, noninvasive methods may permanently eliminate behavior associated with ADD in eighty percent of participants. Her present study will examine the effects of background music on the training session.

Dr. Pratt's research—such as the women in childbirth study and the ADD project—take her all over the world lecturing. In 1990 she coordinated a conference at a medical school in Tallinn, Estonia. She has presented results of her research in China, Japan, Argentina, Brazil, Canada, and nearly every country in Europe. Her grandson Robert recently accompanied her to a conference at Tokyo medical College, after which they traveled throughout Japan. (Dr. Pratt, who is now married to an emeritus patriarch in the Church, George Mortimer, takes each of her ten grandchildren at age twelve on vacation to the country of his or her choice.)

As the editor of *The International Journal of Arts Medicine*, a peer-reviewed scholarly journal that includes articles focusing on all the arts, she reviews contributions of caregivers and artists from Tokyo to Tel Aviv.

What motivates Dr. Pratt to dedicate so much of her time and effort to these projects? She has seen the difference music can make to people like Mary (the woman with an astrocytoma), to women in childbirth, and to so many others who suffer. Acknowledging that music alone is not the cure for all illness, she says, "It's a key to the puzzle. It's a very important tool that sustains many people. I don't discount the advances of medical knowledge and understanding—not at all. But I think that we can pool the insights of arts therapists and arts medicine specialists with more traditional approaches and come up with remedies that are better for everybody."

Reflecting on her own illness, Dr. Pratt comments on the driving force behind her work: "I'm very convinced that the major challenges in anyone's life are there for a reason. We're fitting into a much larger plan.

"I don't think any one of us comes into this world to become a harpist or a surgeon or a dancer, or anything else. Those are things we do. But what we are here for is to develop our potential as unique individuals, and that is not necessarily tied to a certain career or a role in life.

"I think if we are not learning what is basic to our mission here, we are redirected. That may be seen as a tragedy. I understand the terrible devastation and frustration of a young person who suddenly can't walk any more or of a great athlete who has a simply insane accident and can't move. My heart goes out to someone who has to travel that road. I'm sure there's a reason, but it's hard to accept—it was hard for me to accept.

"I never would have done any of these things had I continued as a harpist. Never. I think I was supposed to do something else, and so I'm doing it—it's that simple to me."

Barta Heiner

College of Fine Arts and Communications

by

Lauren Comstock Rogers

Barta Heiner, of BYU's Theatre and Film Department, is an award-winning teacher and actress. This account of Barta's journey, up to and including her years at BYU, depicts a life of creativity and achievement in her field, faith in seeking divine guidance, and dedication in living gospel principles.

*B*arta Heiner didn't get started in theatre until high school and college. She had performed in plays for her stake, school, and such roadshows as *Ponce de Leon Finds the Fountain of Youth on the Moon*. However, she became "officially" involved with theatre because her teachers and mentors often believed in her talent more than she did herself.

Barta was born February 7, 1949, in Ogden, Utah, to H. Bartley and LaVerne Farr Heiner. She has one brother and three sisters. When she was a junior in high school, many of Barta's friends were auditioning for the school play and encouraged her to come. But at first she was too shy. "They told me there was a role in it for a Swedish nurse. Since I did accents pretty well, I waited until everybody was gone and then auditioned for the show. I got the part as the nurse."

"Later I did a play for a state competition and was cast as Grandma in the play *The Sandbox*. I was supposed to play an eighty-year-old woman—my drama teacher spent hours after school coaching and encouraging me because, as she told me, 'I know you can do this.'" Barta performed in the play at BYU, and after the performance, "this 'huge' guy came backstage and said, 'I don't know who gave you permission to start the play, but only half the judges were here, so you're either disqualified, or you'll have to do it over again.' We decided to do it again." Barta won Best Actress in her role as Grandma at that competition. The "huge" man turned out to be Dr. Charles Whitman, who later directed Barta in two plays, both of which earned her BYU Best Actress awards.

Barta attended Weber State College for two years and then decided to transfer to BYU. She received her degree in 1971 in Speech and Dramatic Arts. After she graduated, she went to Los Angeles to act.

In Los Angeles, Barta struggled to get cast. "It's the vicious cycle where you have to have a union card and an agent to get in to audition. But an agent won't look at you unless you've been in a show, which you can't get into unless you have a union card and an agent." After about two and a half years, several of Barta's friends from Utah encouraged her to start a theater with them. She wasn't sure she wanted to return to Utah at that point, so she prayed for help with the decision.

"Some people pray and get bolts-out-of-the-blue kind of answers. With me it doesn't work that way. I do have terrific hindsight, however, and can see how God has directed me away from some very precarious situations." She discussed this matter of getting answers to prayers with her father once, and he said, "God gave you a brain and expects you to use it to work things out." So, because her thoughts kept vacillating about whether to return to Utah, Barta decided to audition for Lizzie, the "old maid," in *The Rainmaker*, and if she didn't get the part, she would go back to Utah. She didn't get the part. A woman who was known for working in pornographic films was chosen.

After working on the theatre project in Utah for the summer, Barta decided to audition for a master's program at the American Conservatory Theatre in San Francisco. She was accepted. She remembers those years as both the best and the worst three years of her life. For her master's thesis, Barta had to write a one-person play. She had been thinking about whom she would base her show on when her family sent her a book written about her great-great grandfather, Lorin Farr. He was the first mayor of Ogden, Utah, and one of Joseph Smith's bodyguards.

All that was said in the book about one of Lorin's sisters, Diantha, was that she didn't like the smell of soap. Barta wondered why more wasn't written about her, so she asked her parents if they could do some more research. They sent her materials from the Daughters of the Utah Pioneers and other historical sources. Barta based her one-person show *Diantha* on this unknown female ancestor by creating the character as a compilation of many women she had read about.

At the time Barta was writing the play, a tragedy happened in her family—a cousin was raped and murdered. While she was walking home from a final exam, she was kidnapped in broad daylight near the LDS Business College in Salt Lake City. This experience directly influenced three small sections of *Diantha*: "It became more clear— it became more 'home-based,'" explains Barta. But, in a more general way, this cousin's death made the writing of her play more personal and emotional. After completing *Diantha*, Barta received her M.F.A. from the conservatory in 1977 and taught part time in the Theatre Department at BYU for two and a half years.

After the loss of her mother from a car accident, Barta became part of a theatre group working to establish a Shakespearean Festival. Unfortunately the festival started to fold because of mismanagement of funds, a matter of frustration for Barta since the producer of the show had said, "You can trust me; I'm a Mormon." His unintentional hypocrisy left everyone involved in the project—nonmembers and members alike—with bad feelings.

Yet the experience had a silver lining. Several of her friends at the Shakespearean Festival knew Barta had done a one-person show and asked to see her perform *Diantha* for the group. Since Barta had tried to write *Diantha* with a universal appeal, so that even people who are not members of the Church would be able to appreciate and understand it, she agreed to perform the play for this mixed audience.

The stage had been set for *A Midsummer Night's Dream*, so Barta had to improvise. That night she appeared as Diantha, with a card table, folding chairs, and Tupperware as her props. "There was a strange, almost scary, feeling in the audience because or the company's animosity toward Mormons. And some members of the company had brought a case of beer with them. I don't think they disliked me—although I'm sure some thought I was a bit strange. They just didn't like Mormons."

"At the beginning of the show, Diantha makes cornbread, and of course one of the ingredients is an egg. When the egg started to roll off the table, I was talking about the young boy who had his hip shot off during the Haun's Mill Massacre. It just so happens that the pioneers treated him with a poultice made of herbs, one of which was slippery elm. So, I was talking about slippery elm right when I leaned over the table to snatch the rolling egg before it went over the edge. The audience burst out laughing, dispersing a lot of the animosity that had been there. The atmosphere warmed and the audience was receptive to the rest of the show." In fact, some people even came up after the show to thank Barta for helping them find God again or feel a spirituality again in their lives.

After the Shakespearean company folded, Barta withdrew for a while. It was a dark time in her life. She felt responsible for having involved her friends in a company that had failed. After about six months of living off her savings because she was unable to find a job, she went to see a counselor. "I suppose I could have wandered in the woods with my dogs for the rest of my life, but I finally went in for some help."

She told her counselor the entire story and how she felt responsible for the company's failure, to which the counselor responded with a meaningful analogy. She suggested that Barta was like a bird on the edge of a cliff, saying, "I've got to fly, I've got to fly." But she couldn't fly yet, because her wings had been terribly damaged. She then suggested that Barta sit back, enjoy the sunset, and wait for her wings to heal and the sun to come back up.

"Just having her say that was a release for me because suddenly it was okay to have failed. I had harbored a lot of anger toward the producer—and the whole situation. We had such a fine company. I was also still angry over my cousin's murder. I had to finally let that anger go and let God take care of it. You can't hold all that inside you because it eats you up and makes you unable to function—you can't think right."

When BYU later asked Barta to come work for them full time, she was acting with the Denver Center Theater Company and teaching at the National Theatre Conservatory there. "I didn't want to go back; I liked what I was doing. I was acting with a professional company and liked it. It was an ideal situation." She told BYU "No," but a few months later, when they called again, she told them she would think about it.

Barta started praying about the decision. She had a feeling she should go, but because she doesn't always feel she gets straight answers to prayers, she wondered if her feelings were more a sentimental response than a spiritual prompting. "Finally this thought came to me one day: You're teaching many people who don't have strong moral convictions to succeed, but maybe it's time to help the ones trying to be good to succeed. So that's why I came back."

Barta began at BYU in January 1988 as an assistant professor in the Theatre and Film Department. Lael Woodbury, a prominent professor in the department, was still teaching when she arrived. He said something to Barta that helped and comforted her: "Whether you made the right decision or not, whether you followed a spiritual prompting or an emotional impulse, if you had righteous desires in what you did, the Lord will bless you."

Shortly after her arrival at BYU, Barta learned that a new script of the Hill Cumorah Pageant was to be produced. She felt prompted to ask the artistic director, Charles Metten, if she could help in any way. He told her that all the positions were filled. "I was disappointed and wondered if the prompting I had received had been just an emotional desire to become involved in a project that was very important to me," she says. However, a few weeks later Dr. Metten informed Barta that one of the assistant directors had dropped out and asked her if she was still available. She accepted and was involved as an assistant or associate director of the new Hill Cumorah Pageant in New York for three years.

Many would have to agree that Barta made a good choice in returning to BYU and has been blessed for it. While at the university, Barta has been the recipient of many teaching awards including a Karl G. Maeser Distinguished Teaching Award in 1992. She is currently an associate professor in her department. In addition to many performances on the radio, on cassettes, and in videos and commercials, Barta has performed in more than twenty-five films, including *A More Perfect Union* in 1988. She has also performed in more than sixty theatre productions, such as *The Glass Menagerie*, *The Rainmaker*, and *The Madwoman of Chaillot*. Barta has also directed fifteen BYU productions, including *Separate Tables*, which was performed November 1996. Other BYU plays she has directed include *Guys and Dolls*, *Pygmalion*, *Hedda Gabler*, and *Jane Eyre*.

Barta Heiner's road before coming to BYU to teach took her many places—Arizona, Colorado, California, and Canada. At times she experienced failure and, at other times, was unsure of the next step to take. Yet all who know her would have to agree that her life course and service at BYU are powerful testaments to Dr. Lael Woodbury's words of encouragement to Barta: "If you have righteous desires in what you do, the Lord will bless you."

Martha Moffitt Peacock
College of Fine Arts and Communications

by
Camille Hally

Martha Peacock has been on the faculty of BYU's Art Department since 1987. A professor of art history with a specialty in northern baroque art, Martha is especially interested in women artists from this period. She has served as an important role model and mentor for women at BYU who are pursuing educational goals while beginning or continuing to care for families. She and her husband, Gregory, have both earned doctoral degrees and taught while raising their five children together.

*T*he young girl looked up at the Angkor Wat temple in amazement. How beautiful the stone walls looked in the sunrise. The effect was magical as the sun successively appeared through the temple's series of doors. She felt a certain excitement stir within her and longed to stand in that spot in Cambodia experiencing this beauty for hours, but her family had started to leave the site. Reluctantly she followed, yet she kept looking back over her shoulder. She has never stopped looking back.

More than a love of art was born within Martha Moffitt Peacock on that day when she was a seventh grader and on a family stay in Thailand and Cambodia. That day marked the beginning of a passion that would later lead to goals requiring great determination to achieve.

Martha Moffitt Peacock was born on February 22, 1957, to John Weldon and Helen Rose Snowberger Moffitt. Martha's mother, Helen, had been brought up in an artistic family and had learned to love drawing. This love naturally played a large part in Martha's interest in art during her early years. Because her family traveled a great deal, Martha's love of art developed further as she was introduced to more and more art in museums all over the world. She has many early memories of living in Germany where she loved to visit art museums. She would often go with her sister, who would take along her humanities book. The two would sit on a bench together and study the many art works around them.

After Martha graduated from high school, she attended Brigham Young University, where she was a participant in the BYU Study Abroad program in London. This was when her love for art really blossomed—she would spend hours at the National Gallery and the British Museum. These experiences led her to choose art history as a major.

The next significant event in Martha's life was her marriage to Gregory J. Peacock. Together they moved to Ohio where they both attended graduate school at Ohio State University. Fortunately, they both received fellowships, which helped them financially with their growing family. Martha and Gregory not only both received Ph.D.s in Ohio—Martha in northern baroque art and Greg in political science—

but they also had two sons and a daughter. After receiving her degree, Martha was offered a full-time teaching position at Brigham Young University. Currently a full-time professor with tenure, Martha now has five children and, as always, a supportive husband. She also continues to be an active member of The Church of Jesus Christ of Latter-day Saints.

At the core of every success in her life has been Martha's passion for what she loves and believes in and her strength and determination through struggle. Her greatest difficulties came when she and her husband were both in graduate school, with children. Martha remembers sitting down with Greg to plan their school schedules. It was important to both of them that one parent always be home with the children, and they planned accordingly. Although the juggling was difficult, Martha remembers that these were also times of joy for her family.

One of the greatest blessings resulting from the Peacocks' decision to study together and share in the caring of their children has been the unity and growth in their relationship. Martha sees some couples struggle as the husbands study, work in professions, and encounter many interesting people and ideas while the wives feel isolated and distanced from their husbands' lives. Because of this, she feels grateful for the time when she and her husband worked through graduate school together while meeting their children's needs.

Martha sought a lot of spiritual strength in those times. During her Ph.D. exams she was often able to recall information more easily after fervent prayer. She also feels she was blessed whenever she made a special effort to spend a lot of quality time with her children. Heavenly Father's help always made things go more smoothly for their family.

Even more difficult for both Martha and Gregory was the three-month period Martha spent alone in the Netherlands doing research for her Ph.D. When she left, her two boys both got the chicken pox, and she was pregnant with her third child. All her professors told her she would need to spend at least a year doing her studies in the Netherlands—that it would be impossible to complete her work in three months. Martha knew, however, that she couldn't spend an

entire year away from her family, so she found a way to do the work
more quickly. With no breaks at all, she spent every one of those long
days in archives and museums until closing time. She is grateful for
the help she received from the local bishop and his family, with whom
she stayed while doing her research in The Netherlands. Upon her
return and the completion of her Ph.D., Martha's hard work paid off
when, in 1987, she was offered a full-time teaching position in the Art
Department at BYU.

One of Martha's areas of focus has been women in art from the
northern baroque period. Considering herself as much a cultural historian as an art historian, she has also studied Dutch literature, history, and music from this period. Much of her time has been spent
studying the female artist Geertruydt Roghman, a seventeenth-centu-
ry Dutch printmaker. Roghman was one of the first artists to illustrate
domestic scenes of women in the household. Martha loves these
works because they represent how the Dutch culture of this time
revered women, home life, and motherhood. Although Martha recognizes that some contemporary women and art historians may not be
drawn to the household and mothering roles represented in these
works—or may even view them as roles that undervalue women—
she personally feels that these women were highly esteemed in their
society and that many today also recognize the supreme value of the
homemaker. She believes that the most important work a woman can
do is in the home with her family. Those relationships should come
above all else.

As a teacher, Martha feels strongly that students should always
approach their studies with a searching mind. They should challenge
the things they learn and always place the gospel at the core of their
search for knowledge and truth. In other words, everything an individual learns should be tempered with what she knows to be right.

Martha serves as a wonderful role model at BYU; she is a successful woman professor who is married, has children, and has a testimony of the gospel. She remembers that she didn't know anybody
like that to look up to when she was a student. Because of her example and her ability to balance so many things successfully, Martha has
young women come to her office many times a day to ask for advice.

She worries that many girls at BYU might give up on their schooling or quest for knowledge if they don't have mentors or see examples of women who have emphasized both family and education in their lives and have stayed true to their dreams. In these dreams, Martha feels a young woman must have confidence in herself and be able to discuss her feelings with her partner.

Martha's example and her dedication to her goals have touched and helped many lives. Her students rave about her teaching and have been touched by her example and patience in helping them plan their own goals.

But most important is how blessed her husband and children feel to have her. The Peacocks are a close family. The children love to learn and go to art museums. They are fluent in German and are starting to study French, and, because of their parents' interests in art history and political science, they have developed a deep love for all kinds of history. The whole family was blessed by an opportunity to live in Vienna during a BYU Study Abroad program for which Martha and Greg taught. In the past, Greg has taught for the Political Science Department at BYU. Currently, he is pursuing his own research while taking care of family and home.

When one talks to Martha Peacock about her life, the most touching aspect is her expression of thankfulness for her husband. She has only been able to do the things she has because of his dedicated support. They both decided, early on, that they would help and support each other in all their individual goals throughout their life together. They have seen many rich personal rewards and blessings in their family by keeping this promise they made to each other before their marriage.

Mae Blanch
College of Humanities

by

Susan Ream

The BYU English Department has consistently been one of the largest departments on campus. Mae Blanch has served the university and students in this department for many years. She brings a world of experience into her teaching and other responsibilities, and one of her greatest gifts, her organizational ability, has brought many students, faculty, and alumni together in meaningful gatherings and relationships over the years. Mae is both logical and tenacious, which means that anything she does, she does well and completely. Sometimes this means she is still up at 3:00 a.m. finishing a jigsaw puzzle.

*N*o one could call Dr. Mae Blanch wishy-washy. Her firm chin and direct look are symbolic of the clarity, the decisiveness, yet the kindliness of her adherence to moral principle. Her life exemplifies persistence and achievement in the face of difficulty.

Born May 11, 1928, in Ogden, Utah, as the third child of Wheatly L. and Florence Eunice Palmer Blanch, she was named Mable for two aunts, but from childhood has always been known as "Mae." Her father died when Mae was fourteen months old; her young mother managed somehow to keep the farm at Plain City, Utah, and, with some assistance from family, to raise her children alone. "I suppose we were poor," Mae says, "but we didn't know it; no one else had very much either."

One of her earliest memories is of a favorite activity—reading. In the 1930s children read "Big Little" books and Mae remembers her sense of accomplishment at reading one called *Little Orphan Annie*, her first book. The future English teacher's favorite activity was taking a book with her and climbing a tree to read, where her mother couldn't find her.

Another early love was for animals; as a child she loved the chickens, the kittens, the rabbits, the horses, the dog, the cows indiscriminately. Her students have encountered the two dogs she has owned since coming back to BYU—Schatzie, and after Schatzie's death, BiBi (for black and brown). Once a student was overheard holding up a returned essay to a friend with the laconic comment, "paw print." And her neighbors are familiar with the regular sight of Mae, book in hand, walking nearby with a small black dog on a leash.

She attended BYU from 1946 to 1950, graduating with a major in English, a minor in German, and went on to teach junior high for two years in Magna, Utah. An opportunity to work in Washington, D.C., brought her east for several years, where she worked for the Department of the Interior, for Senator Dworshak of Idaho, and later for Senator Watkins of Utah.

While in Washington, she faced a major setback when she was diagnosed as suffering from juvenile onset diabetes. She refused to be daunted, but set out to learn to inject herself with insulin, to follow the rigid diets, and to continue to enjoy life. Friends from those years remember her rushing to work, peanut butter and toast (the last item of a "good" breakfast) in hand as she boarded her streetcar. Her energy, her creative gifts (she was in great demand when the old MIA roadshows needed writing), her skill as a seamstress (she often sewed complex Vogue patterns for herself), and her cultural interests in stage plays are still fondly remembered. One friend was particularly awed at her goal of reading Carl Sandburg's several volumes on the life of Lincoln. Mae was one of the leaders in a house of ten young women, and the cleaning and household organizational patterns she established there still continue in the lives of some of those who lived with her.

At mid-school-year, in January, 1958, she returned to BYU to teach. After a year and a half, although enjoying teaching very much, she chose to go to graduate school at the University of Colorado for three years on a National Defense scholarship, finishing her Ph.D. program with a one-year scholarship from the university. She graduated in 1966 in English with a strong interest in comparative literature. Her dissertation on the picaresque novel emphasized *The Tin Drum* by Günter Grass and *The Travels of Augie March* by Saul Bellow.

As a BYU professor with four different classes to teach, and thus four preparations, Mae often found herself working late in her office until 1:00 a.m. or so, and returning at 6:00 a.m. the next morning. One night she locked herself out of her office. While looking for a janitor, she also managed to get locked out of her building! Finally, she tracked down a security man at the old Joseph Smith Building. "Oh, you must be Professor Blanch," he said. She was highly impressed by such precise awareness of who was likely to be working late.

In the English Department, Mae's first, and longest, assignment was to serve as advisor to the English Literary Society, the organization for English majors and other interested students. During a fifteen-year period the organization sponsored a self-supporting movie program, which provided the funds for the annual awards banquet, money toward the new library fund, and support for bringing literary speakers like Robert Penn Warren to campus. Eventually this program became today's BYU International Cinema.

To entertain the students, Mae produced some memorable faculty follies during these years. Her small black dog, Schatzie, made a vivid appearance in red scarf and glasses at one show. Schatzie liked the applause so much she kept trying to sneak back on-stage, with an energetic Dr. Blanch in hot pursuit. The roar of approval from delighted students encouraged Schatzie to keep trying to the point that she developed a permanent addiction to public adulation.

Mae Blanch has served under five BYU presidents—Wilkinson, Oaks, Holland, Lee, and Bateman—and has functioned on many committees at the department, college, and university levels. Mae has many organizational skills, with both an eye to the overall picture and a practical awareness of what is possible. Her gifts have been valuable in many different settings. Her university service has included terms on the presidential scholarship committee, the retirement committee, the degrees for independent study committee, and the university committee on advancement and tenure. At the department level she chaired the committee for recruitment and promotion. Although it may be only a coincidence, she was replaced by two associate chairs!

She also served her community on the Utah County Planning Commission from 1973–76. She remembers working with the commission to preserve the beauty of the Provo Canyon, and helping evaluate developers' plan for future recreation and skiing on the Provo mountains.

Mae has enjoyed working to create special classes. One such class dealt with the mystery novel as a genre. At another point, she team-taught an honors class on the family in fiction. Over the years, students have appreciated the depth and scope of her teaching and have shown their approval in many ways. She was Professor of the Year in the English Department in 1985 and received the Alcuin Award in general education for 1991–94. The award she will never forget came one year when she went to give a final examination to her European novel class—and was presented with a dozen red roses by the class.

Commitment to teaching has been matched by a deep commitment to the gospel. Mae Blanch has filled many ward and stake positions; she was a member of the gospel doctrine writing committee for several years and wrote the entry on prayer in the *Encyclopedia of Mormonism*. She has been an active and energetic member of every ward she has lived in, although this has not always been easy for her—at times problems with her health and the pressures at home and work have caused difficulties. True, she is something of a perfectionist, and thus her high standards are sometimes a scourge to herself and others. But she is also a perfectionist with a sense of humor—and a survivor.

Mae's scholastic and Church service have also expanded to a very human level of love for her students. She became good friends with one young woman who served as an officer in the English Literary Society for which Mae was the faculty advisor. Mae offered her home as a Provo location for the student's wedding, and at the birth of the young couple's first child, Mae decided to make a "christening" dress. Inserted in the dress was some intricate and exquisite handmade lace. This gift represented the love Mae must have felt for many students. Although Mae is not a mother herself, she has indeed extended her love to countless students over her thirty-plus years of teaching at BYU. Her life is an illustration of service, love, and commitment.

Susan Elizabeth Howe

College of Humanities

by

Maralyne Howe and Carri Jenkins,
with material from Susan Howe

Susan Howe's accomplishments are being recognized in the literary world: she has been the editor of Exponent II and managing editor of The Denver Quarterly; her play Burdens of Earth has been performed at BYU; and her poems have appeared in The New Yorker, Literary Review, Southwest Review, Shenandoah, Tar River Poetry, Prairie Schooner, and other journals.

*S*itting in church on a warm August Sunday morning, Maralyne Haskell Howe realized that her longed-for infant wanted to enter this world. Elliot, her husband, drove her to the Provo Medical Center where their first baby, Susan, was born with dispatch. The date was August 29, 1949. Eighteen months after Susan's birth, another child arrived, but when Susan was only two years old, the child died. This sad event repeated itself two more times in the Howe family. Still, Maralyne busied herself with her first-born and, among other things, read her daughter many books. Then, to Maralyne's surprise, Susan read the stories back to her mother with amazing accuracy. In reality, Susan had probably memorized them, but she must have *thought* she was reading.

When Susan entered the first grade, her teacher recognized her academic ability and suggested she be placed in the second grade. Susan had no difficulty with the more advanced curriculum, but struggled socially. In the third grade she started keeping a diary. "The girls were not very nice to me today. I must try to be more kind and friendly, and try to make myself look prettier so I can be their friend." This was Susan's reaction to the bullying of her classmates. Today, she is surrounded by many friends—at the university and in the Church.

Seven more children came to the Howe family. Susan, of necessity, became the second mother to them all. Besides helping with the children, she worked on the family's one-acre farm north of Pleasant Grove. On the farm were homing pigeons, goats, one calf, and one pig. Susan used her literary ingenuity in naming some of these animals—Samson, Delilah, and Hamlet.

Even with her responsibilities at home, Susan was always an excellent student, particularly when it came to foreign languages. Because her father, Elliot Castleton Howe, served as the foreign-language specialist in the Utah State Office of Education, Susan never lacked for support in learning first Spanish and then French.

Susan's teen-age years included active participation in the LDS Church, including seminary. Of course, she was exposed to the cultural expectation prevalent at that time that all good Mormon girls should marry at a young age—and this was the life she wanted. But her education was important to her, so in May 1966, she graduated from Pleasant Grove High School—at age sixteen—and, in the autumn, enrolled at Brigham Young University.

In 1967, her parents were asked to preside over the Dallas, Texas, Mission. All the children, including Susan, accompanied them to the Dallas mission home. Leading a dual-language mission (English and Spanish) was a heavy responsibility for the president and his wife, so that year Susan cared for the children while her mother traveled with her father throughout the mission. At one point, Susan's father "called" Susan to be a companion to a Hispanic sister until a replacement came. Handling the assignment competently, Susan proselyted among the Spanish-speaking residents for three months.

After one year in Texas, Susan returned to Provo and re-entered BYU. She obtained her bachelor's degree in 1971 with a Spanish major and French minor. "I was really good at picking up languages," she explains. "I had a good ear and could learn just about any accent."

During her undergraduate years, Susan also participated in student-body and Church activities. She served on the Supreme Court of the student-body association and became a very young president of a campus Relief Society. She regrets, however, that she did not try out for two other activities that interested her: dramatics and ballroom dancing. "I'll never know if I could have 'made it' in acting or as a ballroom dancer because I didn't even try. So, I missed two enriching and satisfying experiences."[1] At that age Susan's social confidence was still developing.

Following a trip to Spain after graduation, Susan realized that, although she knew about Spanish and French literature, she was not well acquainted with English and American literature—something she later decided to study.

Susan obtained her master's degree in English and creative writing in 1978 from the University of Utah. Later, in 1989, she graduated with a doctorate from the University of Denver in the same fields. Along the way, she began to write poetry—an art form she believes has been locked away in the ivory towers of academia too long.[2]

Today Susan Howe is an acclaimed poet. But she did not even attempt to write her first poem until rather late in her development. Her early training, however, began on the small, one-acre farm north of Pleasant Grove, Utah. There, Susan says, amidst the fruit trees, homing pigeons, and lambs, she planted the seeds for many of her poems. "This valley, the Utah Valley, is truly my home landscape. This is where I feel at peace. And certainly my experiences here color what I write about and how I write."

Perhaps it is because of this rural upbringing, or her own innate sense of equality, that Susan has long championed the idea that good poetry should be available to all. She is pleased with the rising interest in poetry that can be found in such diverse locales as the Cowboy Poetry Festival in Elko, Nevada, or the fashionable restaurants in New York City and San Francisco, where patrons read their poems to one another. Susan believes this is exactly where poetry should be—down among the people.[3]

Because she has received critical praise for her poems, it is perhaps somewhat ironic that Susan makes no apologies for her belief that "poems don't have to be perfect to be worth sharing." She stresses that the quality of one's poems is important, but explains that, "until something is done, even poorly—and shared—it cannot be improved."[4]

Claiming that elitism has injured poetry's popularity, Susan says:

. . . the perception of poetry as difficult keeps us away from . . . wonderful contemporary poets. . . . We still think poetry is something to be studied in a university rather than an art form people can share with others. . . .

Also, poetry deals with human experiences at a deeper level—something we are craving right now. So much of our entertainment today, whether on television or the big screen, floats along on a superficial level. I think we are hungry for art that will speak to the depth of our experience, both in terms of joy as well as sorrow and pain. That kind of art really connects us to life and helps us understand our own trials, our own experiences.[5]

In keeping with this philosophy, Susan writes that, for her, every poem begins with experience. And it is this experience that connects the poet to the reader.[6] As an example, Susan's poem, "Nor Am I Who I Was Then" (at the end of this sketch), describes her feelings at returning home to the house in Pleasant Grove where she grew up. The house, she realizes, is not the same house she once knew and loved. But then again, neither is she the same girl she once knew.

A popular teacher in the BYU English Department, Susan is respected by her students not only for her success in writing and publishing poetry, but also for her teaching manner. She encourages her students to share their poetry with one another, be it good or bad. She remembers that in one class she took, one of her poems was ridiculed. The teacher said, "This doesn't sound like it was written during this century. It's a throwback to the 1800s." His comments almost made Susan give up poetry altogether. Years later she says, "Of course, my early poems weren't very good. I was learning to write. I didn't just emerge from a cocoon as a full-blown poet. But I never would have become better if I had let myself quit because my first poems were awful. I have had to work hard for years to become a poet." Because of her early experiences with poetry, Susan is careful to encourage her own students.

Susan loves to write poetry, claiming, "It's the best gift I have, and it's the best thing I can give." But with her teaching it is becoming more difficult for her to find time to write. "'Teaching,' she quips, 'is not a job, it's a way of life.'"[7]

Besides her teaching and writing, Susan also works on many university committees. For some time she was the chair for the English Department on a committee for women's studies. She also serves on the department's creative-writing committee. When she arrived at BYU, she served for three years in planning the annual BYU Women's Conferences. Her committee members say she is easy to work with—cooperative and thoughtful. She states her feelings clearly, but always with diplomacy.

Following these women's conferences, the talks are always compiled into a book. Susan is proud of the book she edited, titled *Women of Wisdom and Knowledge*, published in 1990 by Deseret Book. In a later conference she also spoke, explaining candidly that, after she first graduated from college, she coasted without any goals:

> . . . I did not know there were any fulfilling, interesting roles a Mormon woman could play except the supposedly all-encompassing role of wife and mother. . . . I can't express how much pain I have suffered between then and now because I did not marry. I wish that someone had taught me that my marital status had nothing to do with my value as a person . . . I wish I could have been open to more possibilities for my future, so I could have felt that, even as I longed for a happy marriage, my life could always be interesting and exciting. . . . So, after college, my life essentially stopped as I waited to get married. . . .
>
> But I have to say that, as I look over my life [after formulating and achieving goals], I'm pretty happy with it. If I consider it as an offering to the Lord, I've done the best I could with the circumstances I have been given. I've tried to grow. I've tried to be a whole person. I've tried to use my talents to serve. I have made some mistakes, but I've also made some significant contributions.[8]

She concluded her talk by stating: "Each woman needs to know that she is unique and that she is of immense worth. And that what she is working towards at any time of her life is of great worth to her and to God."[9]

Although Susan's profession takes up most of her time, she still makes time for friends and some of her favorite athletic activities—skiing, playing tennis, and hiking. On Sundays she enjoys teaching Primary and having supper and playing table games with her family. The Howe family members speak lovingly of how, at Christmastime, when they all draw names to give one gift to another family, generous Susan always gives to everyone.

Susan Elizabeth Howe has been at BYU for only eight years. But in this short time, she has established a reputation as a gifted teacher and a poet of merit. As she continues her teaching, her reputation and her contributions to the university will grow. She will likely be numbered among the best of the Brigham Young University faculty because of her sincere interest in her students and her gift of poetry.

Nor Am I Who I Was Then

Far north in the country
On a clay shelf
Overlooking the valley, the house
Where I was raised holds up
The house you see and
In this way survives
Vagaries of ownership,
History, and reinterpretation.
Once modest, lower middle class
Still it was one of a kind,
Its freshness
Green-speckled bricks
Set in maroon mortar and
Maroon-stained posts and beams
Supporting roof and flat-topped carport

The effect was like silver-
Green pines in red dirt,
Or exotic red-leafed lettuce
They serve in fancy restaurants.
But the roof of tar
Spattered with gravel, roof
Where I myself have walked,
Is dangerous now—pitched steeper,
TV antenna gone—and covered
By standard thirty-year shingles,
Regular and buff as brick
That has grown below
Into sprawling rooms and garages,
Enclosing whole lawns
Of my imagination
                              —Susan Elizabeth Howe

June Leifson
College of Nursing
by
Amy K. Stewart

Since the organization of the BYU College of Nursing in 1952, many deans have worked tirelessly to secure ongoing accreditation from the National League of Nursing. The most recent accreditation (1990) was granted during the administration of Dean June Leifson and was awarded for eight years, the maximum number of years possible. Dr. Leifson, dean of the college from 1986–93, shows great character in an admirable profession. The following article, originally titled "June Leifson: A Nurse by Nature," is reprinted from the February 1991 issue of the Ensign, and is used here by permission.

*A*fter being turned down by three nursing programs at three different universities, June Leifson thought she would never fulfill her dream of becoming a nurse.

"I was turned away because of my speech and my face," explains June, who was born with a severe cleft palate. "One nursing program head even said, 'Oh, no, you could never be a nurse with your speech—and your face would frighten the patients.'"

But June's fighting spirit and determination have enabled her to become not only a nurse but dean of the College of Nursing at Brigham Young University.

Ever since childhood, when she was in and out of the hospital many times for operations, June had wanted to be a nurse. "I saw the compassion of the nurses and the difference a good nurse can make, and I thought, 'Oh, if only I could become a nurse!'"

After being rejected by the universities, June began taking intense speech therapy. "Listening to my voice on tape almost destroyed me, but I never gave up," she remembers. Finally, she was allowed to enter BYU's nursing program on a provisional status, meaning she had to be evaluated every semester to make sure she could "handle it with her speech impediment."

"I really had to prove myself—be a fighter," June says. She graduated from the nursing program, worked at LDS Hospital in Salt Lake City for almost two years, and then went to Hawaii to work as a nurse.

While in Hawaii, June helped start a Primary in a little shack with a dirt floor. With no lesson manual, June prepared the lessons, using Bible pictures she had drawn herself.

One day, while in Hawaii, she was called in to be interviewed for a mission by Elder Spencer W. Kimball. "It was the most spiritual experience of my life up until that time," she says. "Elder Kimball said to me, 'I know you have a speech problem,' and he told me many personal things about his own problem with his voice and cancer."

June served a mission in Japan. She found it difficult at first, but she made up a motto that encouraged her: "If you do your part, God will do his part." She eventually discovered that she could pronounce Japanese more easily than she could English.

After her mission, June earned a master's degree at the University of Michigan and taught nursing at the University of Utah for six years. She earned a doctorate in family studies at BYU, where she became a faculty member, then director of the graduate program in nursing.

The thought of becoming dean never occurred to June. But one day BYU President Jeffrey R. Holland called her into his office and asked her to be the dean of the College of Nursing. "I was petrified," June says. "I didn't know if I could ever do it, but it has been four years now, and I've survived. It's a real challenge, yet it brings me so much joy."

June receives great support from her family. Her parents and five brothers and five sisters have always loved and encouraged her. The Church, too, has been a great help. She has served diligently as a Relief Society president and as a Young Women president, adamantly refusing to let her speech get in the way of her accomplishments.

"I have never married, and I have no children, yet life has been so meaningful," June says. Besides her responsibilities as dean, she keeps busy with her huge garden of herbs, flowers, fruits, and vegetables. She loves to travel and has visited Japan, Israel, and the Soviet Union, among other places.

June has worked hard to overcome her handicap. In the process, she has learned to accept herself. "When I was young, I would pray that I would wake up in the morning and be beautiful and my speech would be perfect," she says. "When I woke up and it hadn't happened, it was very hard on me.

"Then I finally realized that God wanted me the way I was and that I was all right. I can do a lot of good in this life without being beautiful or having perfect speech."

Barbara Day Lockhart

College of Physical Education

by

Jennifer Call

Barbara Day Lockhart represented the United States in speed skating at both the 1960 and 1964 Olympics. After teaching physical education for twenty years at Temple University and the University of Iowa, Barbara began teaching at BYU, where she has also served as a representative to the NCAA, as chair of the Western Athletic Conference, and as president of the Faculty Women's Association.

*R*obert Lockhart was working at the Montgomery Ward department store when he found a pair of speed skates in the basement. He brought the skates home to his eight-year-old daughter, Barbara. At the time, he had no idea what an impact they would have on his daughter's life.

Barbara Day Lockhart was born in Chicago, Illinois, on September 3, 1941. Every winter, a field near Barbara's home was covered with water to make a skating rink. Barbara was trying out her new skates at this rink when Elaine Gordon, the women's national speed-skating champion of the time, saw Barbara and invited her to join the Northwest Speed Skating Club. Barbara accepted and started on the road that would lead her to represent the United States in women's speed skating at the Olympics in both 1960 and 1964.

Barbara's parents, Elizabeth Day and Robert Tilford Lockhart, were both outstanding athletes. Barbara is grateful she inherited her parents' natural athletic abilities and feels indebted to them for their continual support in her athletic endeavors. They never put pressure on her, but rather always gave her confidence. "My father had this vision of me being an Olympic athlete, but there were no Olympic events in speed skating for women at the time—just for men. So he would leave an aisle for me in his garden to practice the long jump."

But it wasn't the long jump that gave Barbara the opportunity to participate in the Olympics. When she was seventeen, just after she had won the national speed-skating championship in her age group, the International Olympic Committee decided to make women's speed skating an Olympic event.

Although she was not even expected to qualify, Barbara went to the 1960 Olympic trials in Squaw Valley, California. She was only in the intermediate division, and there were a lot of women in the senior division that were expected to make the team. The night before Barbara raced, her father assured her that she would qualify for the team. Her father's confidence had such a tremendous effect on Barbara that the next day she not only made the team, she won the race.

Unfortunately, while preparing for the Olympics, Barbara over-trained and got sick. "I had this idea that since I was first in the U.S. I had a good chance to win the gold. Knowing that made me try harder than ever before, and I ended up with mononucleosis. We didn't have trainers or coaches, so we were left on our own—and at the age of eighteen, I didn't use much wisdom. I had to be taken out of the 500-meter race, but I was put in the 1500-meter and finished eighteenth."

Despite her disappointing finish, Barbara was determined to compete again in the 1964 Olympics. She returned home and attended Michigan State University where she could drop out in the winters to train and compete.

Although skating took up much of Barbara's time at Michigan State, she also played on the tennis, lacrosse, and hockey teams, started a women's basketball team, and played the clarinet in the concert band.

During this busy time, a friend sent the Mormon missionaries to Barbara's house. She had been raised in a nondenominational church that did not place any emphasis on doctrine. Her church had told her that God was whatever she thought he was. "In high school I studied physics and chemistry, and it was so clear to me from the natural laws that there had to be a God. I started looking around at other churches and reading all of their philosophies. I finally concluded that no church had the complete teachings of Jesus."

But when the missionaries came, Barbara was so intrigued with what they taught her in the first discussion that she invited them back. As they gave Barbara the rest of the discussions, she learned about fasting and prayer. "I thought I'd try it, and I had a marvelous witness of Joseph Smith being a prophet and seeing Heavenly Father and Jesus; then I raced through the Book of Mormon."

Barbara's testimony grew and she decided to be baptized. However, she found that this blessing didn't come without sacrifice. "I called my parents and told them I was going to be a Mormon. My father and I were really close and had hardly ever differed on anything. But he said, 'If you do that, you can't be in the family.'"

Barbara went to Chicago to be baptized so her parents could attend and see that the Church was something she took seriously. Her father changed his mind and said, " Okay, you can be in this church, but we never want to hear about it." She was baptized in 1963 at the age of twenty-two.

During this spiritually important time of her life, Barbara continued to skate, and she qualified for the 1964 Olympics in Innsbruck, Austria. After dislocating her knee while playing field hockey at Michigan State, she couldn't sprint very well. Instead of giving up, however, she simply concentrated on distance racing. When she went to Innsbruck to compete, she was the best in the U.S. at the 3,000-meter race. Barbara relates the experience that she says was the highlight of her skating career. "That race at Innsbruck was the best race of my life. As I neared the last lap, I was right on the Olympic record and it looked like I was going to win the gold. Then I fell. But it was by far the best I had ever done."

When Barbara returned to Michigan, she resumed her training and began planning for the 1968 Olympics. By this time she had received her B.A. in physical education and was teaching and working on her M.A. in the same field. Unfortunately, Barbara burned her foot just before the 1968 Olympic trials and wasn't able to be on the team.

In 1968, BYU offered Barbara a job as a skating instructor. "I had a research fellowship in Wisconsin to do my doctoral degree in exercise physiology, but when BYU asked me to come, that's what I did. I always pray about where I go, and the Lord makes it so clear where I'm supposed to be."

Barbara worked at BYU from 1968 to 1970 while completing her doctoral work in physical education with a specialty in philosophy. She then spent twenty years teaching at Temple University in Philadelphia and at the University of Iowa in Iowa City.

In 1991 Barbara returned to BYU as a professor in the Physical Education Department, where she currently teaches philosophy classes. These classes deal primarily with ontology, or the nature of being; the meaningfulness of the body; and the worth of the soul—subjects on which she has also done extensive research and publishing. Barbara loves being at BYU because she can use the scriptures and testify of the gospel when she teaches. In 1993, President Rex E. Lee appointed her as the faculty athletic representative to the NCAA (National Collegiate Athletic Association). She has also been the chair of the Western Athletic Conference and the president of the Faculty Women's Association.

Barbara has never married. "For years, I felt like I had done something wrong, but now it's clear to me that this is how the Lord intended my life to be. He has given me so many spiritual experiences to keep me going." Although Barbara didn't choose to be single, she is happy and her life is full of love. Her love for people is evident in the service she has given to the Church and community. She has been on the board of Utah Children, an advocacy board that, among other things, focuses on getting children foster care, and is currently on the boards of Orem, Utah's SCERA (Sharon Cultural Educational Recreational Association) and the local Food and Care Coalition.

With a gift for public speaking, Barbara finds that she can be of further service to others. Her experiences and insights into the gospel have allowed her to share the gospel in unique ways. "My approach to life since I was baptized is to get on my knees and ask, 'What are we going to do next?' The Lord always directs me. I've been able to share the things he has given me and testify of him all the time." Barbara's speaking has taken her throughout the United States and the world. She speaks at professional meetings and organizations as well as for the Church and the Know Your Religion program.

In simple, heartfelt words, Barbara explains why the Lord is so important to her: "I love Him so much, I don't want to be without Him." Her life is an invaluable example of what a person can achieve by centering her life on Christ and filling it with commitment, dedication, and love.

176

Maxine Lewis Murdock

Counseling Center

by

Chad Lewis Murdock and Molly Murdock Broadbent

For a period in the 1970s, Dr. Maxine Murdock was the only woman clinical psychologist in the BYU Counseling Center. Later, two other trained women joined the center: Dr. Della Mae Rasmussen and Beverly Nalder. These women were especially important to the women students on campus and for quite some time were the only women in the center. The BYU Counseling Center gets little publicity, but it can be a tremendous support to any student needing career guidance or emotional support.

*J*t was about eight o'clock in the evening on July 18, 1990, when Dr. Maxine Murdock, a clinical psychologist practicing at Charter Canyon Hospital in Orem, stopped briefly at ZCMI to make a few purchases. While there, she experienced some bewildering physical symptoms. Not wanting to ask for help, she found her way to the car and navigated her way home. As she was leaving her parked car, she collapsed on the cold pavement. A friend, who saw her arrive, carried her into Maxine's condominium and called 911. Maxine's last memory was that of hearing a siren approaching her home.

Maxine was transported to the Utah Valley Regional Medical Center, where at about 4:00 that morning, emergency surgery was performed. Later that day, she was moved to Salt Lake LDS Hospital, where she received more extensive surgery to treat the cancer the doctors had discovered.

Her recuperation was long. Molly, her daughter, had flown from New York City when she learned of her mother's plight. It was perhaps the only period in Maxine's life when she had to be completely dependent on someone else. But because of her daughter's care, modern medicine, and her own will to live, she survived and is now continuing to give the expert advice and encouragement for which she is so well known.

The preparation for imparting this guidance extends far back into Maxine's childhood. In 1926, when Maxine Lewis was only five years old and living in Toppenish, Washington, her father, Sterling Samuel Lewis, died suddenly of pneumonia. This traumatic event prompted her widowed mother, Fern Michie Lewis, to return to Provo, Utah, with her two children, Maxine and Rex.

Maxine remembers her early feelings of loss and sadness and knew, even at that young age, that everyone in the family had been deeply affected by her father's death. The well-intended but misdirected advice of those who tried to console Maxine and her family felt hollow and insincere to a child who knew she loved and missed her daddy. The young family remained in Provo near extended family while Maxine's mother worked to support them. Maxine was painfully aware of her need for both father and mother. Her recognition of such feelings laid a strong foundation for the career path she would choose later in life.

In Provo, Maxine attended Brigham Young Laboratory School from kindergarten through tenth grade. She then moved to Midway, Utah, with her mother, a new stepfather, and four younger siblings. She earned valedictorian honors at Wasatch High School in Heber.

When she returned to Provo to attend BYU, Maxine worked part time as a secretary to pay tuition. Between her studies and work, a friend, John R. Murdock, courted her, and at the end of Maxine's first year of college, they were married. Eventually they became the parents of two sons, Larry and Chad, and one daughter, Molly.

Maxine's years as a young mother were busy. She was actively involved in her children's education, including the development of their musical and artistic talents. She was also called to serve in the ward and stake Primary and Young Women organizations. On occasion, she would even serve as a secretary and bookkeeper in her husband's accounting business.

During this time, Maxine also discovered an important interest, fueled perhaps by her early longing to know more of her father. Maxine started to collect pictures and histories of many ancestors and was soon able to trace back the lines of sixteen ancestors—all of whom had crossed the plains as Mormon pioneers. One ancestor belonged to a handcart company that was so low on food that each person was allowed a scant three tablespoons of flour per day. Gratefully, this company was later rescued. Maxine carefully framed and displayed the pictures she'd collected of her ancestors so her children would know these valiant forebears.

Always an avid reader, Maxine actively sought educational opportunities during these years. While her children were young, she regularly attended BYU Education Week. But this opportunity didn't still her longings for more formal education. She was determined to complete her unfinished bachelor's degree at the first chance.

Finally, at age forty-four, Maxine Murdock returned to BYU as a sophomore. She discovered such a keen fulfillment from her studies in psychology that she knew she wanted an advanced degree. She entered BYU's Ph.D. program in clinical psychology immediately after graduating with her B.A. and quickly gained reputation as a bright, caring, and untiring graduate student. These traits are constant themes in her clinical, teaching, and family life.

After the completion of her Ph.D. coursework, Maxine was hired as a therapist in the BYU Counseling Center. On receipt of her Ph.D., at age fifty-five, she became a full-time faculty member in the Clinical Psychology Department at BYU where she remained until her retirement eight years later. Maxine was highly respected during her tenure at BYU. She was a competent and insightful therapist, a favorite teacher, and a supervisor to many clinical graduate students trying to hone their therapeutic skills. She particularly enjoyed teaching the undergraduate introductory psychology course. (When she returned to BYU as a sophomore this was the course that piqued her own interest in the subject.) Maxine also participated in special university assignments: with the BYU Security Office, the BYU Admissions Office on admissions decisions for emotionally disturbed students, and with Marilyn Arnold, administrative assistant to the president, on the needs and concerns of women faculty and students. As an expert on sensitive family issues, Maxine has been recognized by the Church through its publication of her articles in the Ensign.

How can she integrate student life and psychology work with the responsibilities of home? Maxine's children have many tales to relate. They remember her taping notes of whatever she was studying throughout the house—over the stove, above the kitchen sink, and from the fluorescent desk lamp in her home office. The notes even appeared in church if sacrament meeting ever became dull! One son remembers that Maxine was always available for questions, discussions, and encouragement. Even if doing household tasks, accounting work, or studying, she was never out of earshot of his violin practicing. She corrected the sour notes at times, but always complimented the melodious passages.

Her daughter, Molly Murdock Broadbent, adds some of her own memories:

> As my mom's youngest child, I was in kindergarten when she decided to return to school. We studied together from notes taped to the kitchen curtains while washing dishes and from notes taped to the bathroom mirrors while we combed our hair. I knew school

was important to my mom. She decided she could continue her schooling as long as she could get A's. I knew that if my mother was getting A's, I had to get A's too.

Now as a mother, I realize how difficult it must have been for my mother to successfully be a mom, full-time student, and employee, yet I never felt neglected. As my Beehive advisor, my mom told our class that it is never too late to change your behavior. She slipped her psychological wisdom in between lessons and parties.

When I was in high school, Mom was writing her dissertation as well as working at BYU. Every Thursday she left the house at 5:30 a.m. to drive to Delta to work in their counseling center. Other days, she drove all over Utah, to interview prisoners' families, trying to determine what made the difference in the lives of those who later stayed out of prison. She told me that knowing someone cared was what made the difference in the prisoners' lives. Mom was determined to let those she came in contact with know she cared.

She worked with numerous students, most of them with simple problems, others with serious ones. She frequently counseled them to work closely with their bishops. She also worked with many elders and sisters in the MTC. Some of them were experiencing extreme nervousness as they left for distant lands. Many have acknowledged that they could not have completed their missions without her confidence in them.

Although she was very busy, Mom always attended my school events, hosted my birthday parties, and helped me with homework, even when it meant she was up all night finishing her work. Now she shows the same care by seeing many clients at reduced fees or free of charge. Her reward is the many letters and phone calls she receives from those who want to express thanks for the great help she has given. Former students call and say, "I know your mother won't remember me, but she helped me fifteen years ago. I am in the area today and wanted to say thanks."

In her capacity as a psychologist, Maxine is an excellent listener, is empathetic and kind, and projects hope and optimism. But she is also careful to always confirm her intuition with written clinical examinations. When she detects physical causes in mental health conditions, she always refers these individuals to medical doctors to get appropriate medication.

Maxine counseled BYU students to strive for balance, interspersing their serious study with some relaxation and a few moments of fun. Most of all, Maxine wanted people to be "real" and to succeed, but with humility and balance, within the framework of Christian moral principles. She always loved it when General Authorities would intersperse their doctrinal talks with quick flashes of humor and admit that they, too, were "real" and wrestled with some mild imperfections. She really laughed when one General Authority related that he once discovered a small rip in his trousers and had to ask a secretary if she would quickly mend them so he could keep an important appointment.

Although Maxine has retired from BYU, she has not retired from clinical work. She has continued her career by seeing both inpatients and outpatients at the Charter Canyon Hospital in Orem and Salt Lake City. She has had to cut back a little on her work but still consults with private patients at a newly organized clinic in Orem, Utah.

In addition to her fine reputation as a psychologist, Maxine is also known as a creative cook and gracious hostess who welcomes friends and extended family on holidays and other special occasions. A lover of the beauties in nature, she enjoys caring for the flowers and plants in her yard. She has also enjoyed traveling throughout the western states in her RV. Her family now includes seven grandchildren, each one loved by "Grandma Maxine." Sometimes one or more of her grandchildren will greet Maxine as she returns home from work.

Maxine Murdock's motivation has always been to help others, whether in her family, church service, or career. She exemplifies the deep satisfaction one can gain from a meaningful profession and just how much a woman can do when she enters a career in middle adulthood. But perhaps the greatest indicator of Maxine's character can be seen in her determination to survive her recent bout with cancer, which is also a powerful reminder of the hope she imparts to others.

Lucile Markham Thorne

Library

by

Sally Thorne Taylor and Janice Thorne Dixon

Lucile Thorne was a part of Brigham Young University from her early school days at BYU Training School until her retirement from the library. She contributed steadily to the university's development while successfully rearing five children. In this sketch you will find in Lucile a remarkable example of industry, persistence, and optimism.

*J*n 1929, Lucile Markham graduated from Brigham Young University at the early age of twenty. Immediately she accepted a teaching position at the Juarez Stake Academy in Colonia Juarez, Mexico, teaching high-school students in the subjects of English, dramatic art, and sewing. She taught there happily for two years, all the while corresponding with a missionary who was serving in Great Britain. When her friendship with him had developed into romance, Lucile terminated her teaching and returned home to marry her sweetheart, Harold Arthur Thorne. Five children were born of that union—four daughters and one son.

In March 1941, ten years after the marriage, tragedy struck. Lucile's husband, a sales representative for Hewlett Jams and Jellies, had been traveling in southern Utah. She received two unusual phone calls—one from the police department and another from a reporter. At first, she was unable to completely comprehend the information they were giving her, but she felt something was wrong. Finally she understood that her husband had been brutally murdered by a hitchhiker. Lucile retained her composure outwardly, but inside, she was in complete shock.

Changes had to be made in the Thorne household. Lucile and the five children moved into the home of her mother, Mary L. Markham. Mary performed the domestic services of the home—caring for the children, cooking, and doing housework—while Lucile provided for the financial obligations. Lucile's relationship with her mother was one of the most harmonious and fulfilling relationships of her life. It was one of mutual understanding, respect, and love. In her mother's later years, Lucile took complete care of her until her mother's death at age ninety-six.

Immediately after her husband's misfortune, Lucile accepted a position at the Provo Public Library. Then she worked for six years as a second-grade teacher at Joaquin Elementary School in Provo. Because she loved her library work, however, she later returned to the Provo Library as head of the Children's Department. While there, she organized a successful storytelling program. At this time she also started taking library classes from BYU, and in 1945, accepted employment as a librarian there. In June 1955, Lucile obtained a master's degree in education from BYU, followed by a master's degree in library science from UCLA. Finally, in 1967, she received an Ed.D. from BYU, allowing her to join the graduate school of library science as a professor. She taught classes for both the BYU Library and the Department of Education from 1955 to 1975. Her favorite class was children's literature.

One year, while on leave from BYU, Lucile organized the library at the Provo Central Junior High School. During the summers of 1966, 1967, and 1968, she was a visiting professor at the University of Utah. She was also invited to serve as a lecturer and panelist at the University of London.

Incredibly, Lucile was able to accomplish all this while working to provide a living and home for her family. She remained solvent through it all, without having to borrow or get assistance from others. And she always maintained a beautiful attitude—free from bitterness or self-pity, always hopeful, forward-looking, and enthusiastic.

What kind of background did Lucile come from that enabled her to succeed so remarkably while caring for five little children after the tragic loss of her husband? Clearly her parents must receive much of the credit, for they certainly did lead the way through lives of faith, hard work, and determination.

One Halloween, Joseph and Mary Lewis Markham of Spanish Fork, Utah, were greeted not by goblins, but by an infant daughter, Lucile. Lucile had two older brothers: Joseph Markham, who became an accountant in Oakland, California, and Fred L. Markham, architect, of Provo, Utah. Another brother, Max, died as an infant.

When Lucile was a toddler, her family moved from Spanish Fork, Utah, to nearby Provo, for better opportunities. She remembered riding on the wagon with her doll during the move. For a while, her father worked at the mines in Eureka. During the summer the family stayed there, and Lucile remembered well her father's coming up from the mine covered with black dust. Later, he took a job as an attendant at the State Mental Hospital. As a teenager, Lucile attended dances there and sometimes even danced with the patients. Her stories included some frightening but humorous experiences from those dances.

Both parents provided their children with encouragement to get an education. As a result, all the children later became successful in the professional world. And they all remained true to the tenets of the gospel, which was an important part of their heritage.

Lucile's early schooling was at Brigham Young Training School, which was located two blocks from her home. There she formed life-long friendships with a group of girls—Arlene Harris Grover (daughter of Franklin Harris, then president of BYU), Ethyl Kartchner Tregagle (wife of the principal of Provo High School for many years), Ruth Clark Hafen (mother of Bruce Hafen, formerly BYU Provost and currently a member of the First Quorum of the Seventy), and the late Nita Wakefield Eggertsen, who, until her death, kept a home across the street from lower campus.

According to her diligent nature, Lucile started attending college classes while still in high school, hardly remembering her high school graduation. Her 1929 graduation from BYU, at age twenty, and her two following years as a teacher in Mexico served her well when tragedy struck her family—she had learned to earn a living.

Despite the heavy demands on her during the years after her husband's death, Lucile was careful to make time for her children: Janice, Norma Joyce, Mary Lou, Jim, and Sally. She had the gift of telling a story well. In the evenings the family would sit and talk about Aunt Mag, or Aunt Ret, or Grandfather Stephen, and the people of those stories would come alive.

Lucile's love for her children and grandchildren was wholeheart-ed, but at times she recognized that love must be firm. One time, her grandson, who wanted his way about something, said to her, "Grandma, there's only one thing wrong with you."

"What's that?" she asked.

"You always have to be right."

"That's correct," she retorted. "And that's the way it's going to be."

She got her way, and the grandson had to live with her decision.

During her working years, Lucile was extremely active with Church callings—stake Sunday School and Primary boards, ward and stake Mutual presidents, Junior Sunday School coordinator, and a teacher in various auxiliaries—and served for a time as the president of the Utah Library Association. She also renewed an old love of the theater and acted in several stage plays, including *Arsenic and Old Lace*. After her retirement, she became a professional actress, playing in local motion pictures, on the stage, and for television advertisements. Many people reported seeing her on television—licking an ice cream cone, riding down the road in a recreational vehicle, or sitting on a bus full of coughing people. She can also be seen as one of the supporting actresses in the production, *Mr. Krueger's Christmas*, starring Jimmy Stewart, and in the role of Elizabeth in a BYU film portraying the birth of Christ.

Amazingly, Lucile also continued to work—first full time and later part time—at the BYU library after her retirement. At home she loved handiwork of many kinds, including knitting, crocheting, and quilting. She also loved to work in her yard where she grew a variety of plants.

In 1976, an unusual honor came to Lucile. She was chosen as Utah Mother of the Year and went on to national competition. At the national convention she won the spiritual award for the nation. Throughout her life, she had been optimistic, genuine, and nonjudgmental—qualities the judges and others at the competition recognized immediately.

Lucile loved to travel, and after retirement, she visited parts of the United States, Europe, the Orient, Mexico, New Zealand, and other countries. When she returned home from these trips, she always brought her family members something she had purchased. Once she brought them some opals from Hong Kong.

When she was in her seventies, Lucile and her four daughters went on a trip to Mammoth in California. They went hiking and shopping, and finally the girls talked Lucile into going on a horseback ride. Lucile had ridden a horse when she was younger, but it had been over fifty years earlier. After two hours on the horse, Lucile couldn't get off—her muscles had stiffened, and she couldn't throw her leg over the horse's back. It took her four daughters and several men to help her. She may have been embarrassed, but she was laughing too hard to let anyone know. This was the sense of humor that had helped her so much throughout her life.

When she was eighty years old, Lucile became ill with polymyalgia rheumatica and needed a companion with her. Lenore Heath joined Lucile's household, caring for her for two years, until she passed away on November 29, 1989. After her death, her children discovered her journal, which she had begun keeping after the death of her husband. In it she had corresponded with her husband, telling him of the children's progress, her own attainments, and items she felt he would be interested in. She had kept her love for him alive.

Throughout her life, Lucile Thorne showed outstanding qualities. She based her life on strong spiritual conviction and was willing to use her energy for the good of the community. Admired by everyone for her intelligence, charm, and love, Lucile brought dignity and solidarity to her marriage and family, competence and dedication to her studies and profession, and honor to her rich Utah heritage.

Connie Lamb
Library

by
Janet Porter,
Carolyn Lamb Bean, and Marjorie Wight

Connie Lamb's scholarship on a wide variety of topics is just one of the many assets that make her such a valued reference librarian at BYU. And her most important assignment—setting up the library in the BYU Jerusalem Center—will be a lasting contribution to all who visit there. From this biographical sketch, it is easy to see why this kind and committed librarian is so admired.

*C*onnie Lamb was traveling alone by train through East Germany. Her destination was Berlin, at that time an oasis in the middle of communist East Germany. The countryside around her was silent, drab, depressing. A soldier, checking identification, clicked his heels and gave a "Hitler salute." Chills went up Connie's spine. She became even more apprehensive when she arrived at the Berlin train station and saw guards almost everywhere holding weapons. At length, when she spotted a group of fellow missionaries waiting for her, her relief knew no bounds.

Connie's arrival in Berlin, her last city during her service in the North German mission in the mid 1960s, was so frightening that the memory has remained one of her most vivid recollections over the years. In fact, her entire mission experience was memorable, but for a different reason. Before her mission, Connie had studied another foreign language, but not German. Still, Connie responds to challenges, and learning the German language was just that—a real challenge. It is exactly this readiness for a challenge that has helped her over the years to respond to other difficult assignments and situations.

Connie was born in the late 1940s as the sixth child to Delbert and Alta Wright Lamb. The Lambs must have sensed that this would be their last child, because Connie became the "bright spot" in their lives. The family home where Connie lived all her growing-up years was in Bountiful, Utah. Both her mother, a former school teacher, and her father, a school principal for many years, encouraged her in her scholastic endeavors. The atmosphere at home was definitely one of learning.

It is not surprising, then, that Connie excelled primarily in academics during her years at Stoker Elementary School and Bountiful Junior High and High Schools. But she also developed a fondness for sports, particularly basketball and baseball. After graduating from high school, Connie's love of the outdoors prompted her to earn a B.S. from the University of Utah in biology and an M.S. in botany and plant ecology. To earn money during these years, she worked part time in the University of Utah Marriott Library.

After Connie returned from her mission to Germany, her career plans changed as she launched into yet another challenge. She realized that she enjoyed the atmosphere of libraries so much that she decided to seek a master's degree in library science at Brigham Young University. Graduating in April 1977, she was BYU's co-valedictorian.

After a few years as a reference librarian at the Salt Lake City State Library, Connie returned to BYU in December 1979, as head of the on-line search services at the Harold B. Lee Library. Here she quickly established a reputation for thoroughness and competency in her work. And her students and co-workers know her to be kind and patient. In addition to her library jobs, Connie has had other professional obligations: she served as the coordinator of the 1979 Utah Governor's Conference on Libraries and as a member of the Advisory Committee on Libraries from 1979 to 1986.

However, Connie's life at BYU has not been all library work. She also volunteered for three years teaching English to Asian refugees and then went back to school part time to fulfill another goal—in 1987, she received an M.A. degree in international relations with an emphasis on the Middle East.

While working on this degree, and quite unknown to her, Connie was preparing for her most important job. In Israel, the Jerusalem Center was beginning to be built—with great excitement. To her surprise, Connie was asked in the autumn of 1987 to organize the library at this new center for Near Eastern studies. Her acceptance of this assignment was clearly a continuation of her lifelong determined response to a challenge.

Before the completion of the Jerusalem Center, the BYU students in Israel had been living in a Jewish Kibbutz, Rame Ramet Rachel. They had access to some improvised library facilities there which contained many books on biblical studies and the history and geography of the Palestinian area—but the books had never been categorized. So, when the Jerusalem Center was completed, two large rooms were set aside to house these books. Thus, the BYU Jerusalem Center library was born, and it was Connie's task to organize it.

She began this large task by separating the books into different categories: books on biblical studies, books by LDS authors, books by non-LDS scholars, books on the history of the Arab and Jewish conflicts, and books pertaining to the geography of the area. She then photocopied the title pages and returned them to the BYU Lee Library where they could be officially catalogued.

During Connie's stay, David Galbraith and Martin Hickman, the BYU Jerusalem Center teachers, often spoke of the miracles that occurred time and again as the Church leaders planned for and built this center. After five years and considerable prayer and work, leaders were finally able to obtain the property—one of the best pieces of land in Jerusalem. Guiding and supervising the efforts were President Howard W. Hunter, of the Quorum of the Twelve, and President Jeffrey Holland and Brother Fred Schwendiman of the BYU faculty.

The center was built as quickly as possible amid great controversy and opposition from orthodox Jews. They staged protests and wrote letters and articles against the Church's building plans. Finally, an agreement was reached which allowed the Church to complete the center. This building provides students and faculty with a beautiful environment in which to study one of the world's most crucial political and religious areas.

Connie remained in Israel for six months and, when not involved with the library, traveled on field trips with the students—a real highlight for her after her studies on the Near East. She especially loved her visits to the sites of biblical passages, as well as her two-week stay in Galilee, where she studied the life of the Savior. Also memorable was a Christmas party at Shepherd's Field, when the group, looking toward Bethlehem, sang Christmas carols. And Church meetings, held on Saturdays, were always uplifting.

Because Connie lived at the center, she was able to enjoy the constant association of the students and staff and eat the wonderful food cooked by the Arab cooks. Interestingly, the security guards at the center were not Arabs, but Jews. The Jerusalem Center, then, is one of the few places in Israel where Jews and Arabs work harmoniously together.

Although Connie's Jerusalem experience has been one of her greatest challenges and highlights, it has by no means been her only professional accomplishment. During her library career, Connie has written several articles for scholarly publication and presentation. She has also co-edited two books. The second book, *Jewish American Fiction Writers: An Annotated Bibliography*, won the Association for Jewish Libraries 1992 Posner Judaica Bibliography Award. In 1990, Connie received the Distinguished Service Award from the Utah Library Association.

Connie is currently a reference librarian and the subject specialist at the BYU library for anthropology, the modern Near East, and women's studies. She also supervises two branch libraries at the BYU Anthropology Museum and the BYU Jerusalem Center. With this second library she must use faxes and electronic mail to communicate with the personnel there.

Always involved in a variety of pursuits, Connie has also taught Book of Mormon classes on campus in recent years and has served as an officer for Phi Kappa Phi and the new Faculty Women's Association. She participates regularly in an amateur archaeology group and a book club. And in addition to all this, Connie is now working on a doctorate in anthropology at the University of Utah.

Although Connie is always punctual and dependable, giving her all to her library assignment, she is sometimes hard to find during the noon hour. But, her co-workers usually know where she is—at home giving her dogs Riley and Missy some attention. Connie likes to relate one humorous experience that happened when she took Riley to the veterinarian for his shots. After the appointment, while she was carrying him out, he wiggled so much that she quickly threw him into the car, along with her purse (and keys), and closed the door. As she walked around to the driver's side, Riley got so excited that he jumped over and, with his paw, came down on the button that automatically locks all the doors. Embarrassed Connie returned to the vet's office to call the police for help.

Connie has consistently served in the Church. She loves to attend the temple, both at home and when traveling. While in college, she was ward and then stake sports director. Some of her other callings include Relief Society and Gospel Doctrine teacher, counselor in a Relief Society presidency, and a consultant in her stake family history center. But some of her most fulfilling experiences have been with the Young Women. She went to girls' camp for several years and later served in a Young Women presidency. A real friend to the girls, Connie spent many hours with them in various sports activities, bike rides, and guitar sessions. Once she hiked with the girls up a mountain in the dark to watch the sunrise from the top.

Connie's love of the outdoors has continued since her youth, when her family spent considerable time in the mountains. Several years ago, she hiked to the top of Mount Timpanogos with a sister, Renee, and her family. And in the summers, Connie frequently joins another sister, Carolyn, and her family at their cabin in Brighton, Utah. Because of her botany background, she tries to identify plants as she hikes. She also grows plenty of plants—a variety of flowers and vegetables—in her gardens at home, a hobby that requires quite a bit of her "spare" time.

Connie is close to her family; she gets together often with her five brothers and sisters and many nieces and nephews for special occasions. When her mother unexpectedly passed away in 1986, Connie felt a great loss. At this same time she was asked to assist with the library at the Jerusalem Center, an assignment which she fulfilled with determination in the face of her loss. Connie has never backed away from a challenge.

Jan Porter, a colleague, provides us with some personal feelings about this outstanding librarian: "Connie Lamb is wonderful to work with—she's always kind and considerate and treats everyone with respect and patience. I especially appreciate her willingness to train new students, which requires her to explain things again and again." Dan W. Hone, administrator at the Jerusalem Center, adds some final words of endorsement:

Connie helped make the library in the Jerusalem Center not only a functioning facility for students, faculty, and staff, but also a showplace. Last year we had nearly 74,000 visitors at the center who saw the library as part of their visit. This year we expect that number to increase. Connie continues to be instrumental in helping us with acquisitions and administrative support. We are grateful she is one of the pioneers who has helped in the establishment and continued growth of this center.

Mary Ellen Edmunds
Missionary Training Center
College of Nursing

by

Sandra Rogers and Mary Ellen Edmunds

Anyone associated with missionary work for The Church of Jesus Christ of Latter-day Saints has heard of Mary Ellen Edmunds. But some do not know that besides being a director at the Missionary Training Center, she received her registered nursing degree from the BYU College of Nursing in 1962. She also taught nursing at BYU for five years. Her professional training, enthusiastic personality, firm testimony, and love of people have suited her for the repeated human-

itarian missions she has served in distant parts of the world. Here Mary Ellen tells her own story, which is preceded by remarks from Sandra Rogers, dean of the College of Nursing when, in April of 1994, Mary Ellen received the BYU Presidential Citation.

*K*nown to hundreds of missionaries and thousands of members around the world, Mary Ellen Edmunds has truly spent her life on God's errand "to comfort the weary and strengthen the weak."

Mary Ellen's altruistic instincts were realized in her 1962 degree in nursing from BYU. Soon after her graduation, she was called to the Southern Far East Mission. She was one of the first sister missionaries in the Philippines. She then returned to a faculty position in the BYU College of Nursing, where her wit and wisdom touched the lives of many nursing students. Mary Ellen always acts on the truth that we must esteem one another as ourselves.

It seems incongruous that the unassuming Mary Ellen would be "a first" so often, but in 1972 her second mission call came; this time as one of the Church's first health missionaries. She returned to the Philippines to begin strengthening the spiritual and temporal lives of the Saints she loved so much. One Filipino mother told her, "If only you had been here before, I wouldn't have lost other babies. Thanks to you, I'm going to have a healthy Mormon baby now." That Mormon baby, named for Mary Ellen, is now twenty-one years old.

Mary Ellen was the heart and soul of the health missionary program in those early developmental years. She served as the coordinator of health missionaries for two years, preparing hundreds of instructional and motivational aids.

Never tempted by the honors or security of traditional professional practice, Mary Ellen's work for the last sixteen years has been as a director of training at the Missionary Training Center (MTC). Hundreds of couples, elders, and sisters have been lifted and sustained by her words and example.

Mary Ellen received the BYU Distinguished Alumni Service Award in 1982 and the Exemplary Womanhood Award in 1984. In

1986 she received the Brigham Young University Academy of Medicine's Humanitarian Award for "unusually distinguished service in alleviating human suffering and contributing to the well-being of the world family." In 1986, she was called to the Relief Society General Board after having, she says, only one other Relief Society calling—that of visiting teacher.

Despite these many honors, positions, and awards, Mary Ellen's heart remains with people like the little Vietnamese girl in a pink sweater she met in a refugee camp in the Philippines or with tiny, thin "Broomstick," the Nigerian girl she often held and rocked in Eket.

Mother Theresa once said of her work with lepers, "when you touch them, you minister to the body of Christ." Mary Ellen has ministered in such a way that the poor, the sick, and the weary have felt the hand of Christ in her touch.

—Sandra Rogers

I was born on fast Sunday. You might say Mom gave tithing "in kind." It was March 3, 1940, in the Good Samaritan Hospital in Los Angeles, California. I don't remember a whole lot about it, and last year when I drove past the hospital, there was no plaque or anything, so I guess it wasn't that big a deal. My father is a doctor and my mother a nurse. I have an older brother, Paul K. Jr., and then after me came Charlotte, Susan, Franklin Middleton, John M., Ann M., and Richard M. All of us have graduated from college and six of the eight have served missions.

We moved to Cedar City, Utah, in 1943 where Dad was a "family doctor." He used to go on house calls around the community and in the Indian village adjacent to our town. Lots of times we would be able to go with him, usually one at a time, and carry his medical bag. Life was pleasant and mainly free from care.

I remember that during World War II, Mom went to work briefly to help train nurse's aides at the Iron County Hospital (one block from our home). That was my only taste of a working mother, and I didn't like it. I liked coming home from school and shouting, "Mom!" and having her answer. I loved it when she made whole-wheat bread and let us eat it when we got home. We'd have a tablespoonful of cod liver oil each day, and orange juice and iodine tablets at school.

Along with being a very busy family doctor, Dad was in the stake presidency for about ten years. That meant he was seldom "free," but he always read to us in the evenings whenever he had a chance; Mom too. On my own, I began reading things like *Cherry Ames, Student Nurse* (then there were twenty-two other books about her and her nursing adventures). Later I got into animal books and books about airplanes and sports. I have always loved books and reading.

Dad taught us a lot about self-defense. He would have us do push-ups. When we could do ten in a row, we got a dollar. He also taught us to box (gloves and all). He and Mom were both concerned about our language and would kindly correct our mistakes. We were also taught table manners—like using a butter knife, no elbows on the table, and don't talk with your mouth full. We followed those rules for quite a few years, then gradually dropped them except for in "formal settings." We didn't have funny books in our home, but were allowed to have the classic comics. Dad would read poems like "Hiawatha" to us until we could almost say them by heart.

Music was an important part of our home life. All of us took piano lessons for varying amounts of time. When I was about nine years old I started on the violin. My teacher was Roy L. Halversen. He was one of the most influential people in my life. He took a tough little kid and injected a love of classical music that has had a profound effect. My sister, Charlotte, studied the cello. At one time Charlotte and I were in four orchestras. Each year, for several years, we got to participate in the annual *Messiah* presentation. Those are marvelous memories.

From the time we were little, we began having "Home Night" once a week. One of the great events was when we were too tall to stand beneath the mantle above the fireplace—then we knew we were growing for sure.

I was a tomboy during those growing years. Life was wonderful. I had lots of places to play and an imagination that never quit working. I had a grasshopper hospital, a cemetery, a high-jump pit—I even trained for the Olympics (in my own imagination, out in a vacant lot near our home), and I'd change events almost weekly. I ran away from home a couple of times. My mom would help me get ready. Once I struck out for California so I could get a horse.

In fifth grade I won a contest for drawing an Easter scene. In sixth grade I was high-jump champion (it wasn't easy to jump higher than the boys!) and was on the boxing and tumbling teams. When I was twelve, I wrote a poem and won sixth place in a contest—I got a pen and pencil set with my name on it. I took ballet, but after two lessons the teacher asked me not to come any more. When I was sixteen and seventeen, I worked at Zion National Park, and that was one of my first experiences at being homesick. I did a lot of hiking and exploring.

Then our family moved to Mapleton. Dad had been investigating jobs in both Utah and California and decided Utah would be a better place to raise a family. He worked at the Health Center at BYU. We went to register at Springville High School, but they said their senior class was full, so Mom took all of us to BY High in Provo. Four of us graduated from that excellent school before it closed in 1968. I was our class valedictorian in 1958. I played every sport I could, but particularly enjoyed basketball, softball (I pitched), volleyball, and track.

After high school I went to BYU, graduating in May 1962 with a B.S. in nursing. I was the speaker at our "White Graduation" and led the class in the Nightingale Pledge. Nursing has been a wonderful profession, and I've never regretted choosing that as my focus. My sister Charlotte graduated within two weeks of me; she had gone to Ricks College, which had a two-year program. We got to work together in the same hospital a few times.

In 1962, about the time we graduated, I received a mission call— Southern Far East. I told my Mom I was going to Florida, but she knew it was a little farther than that. After a week in the Missionary Home in Salt Lake (no language training), I was on the airplane headed for an overnight stay in Tokyo and then on to Hong Kong and the beginning of a two-year mission. I spent four months in Taiwan, five months in Hong Kong, then was sent to the Philippines for fifteen months. My companion and I were the first lady missionaries to go there. There was one branch and fewer than a hundred members. We worked hard! What a marvelous place!

When I returned home, I taught nursing at BYU for five years. I became a supervisor at Utah Valley Hospital for two years. During this period I served a two-year stake mission at BYU and taught at the Missionary Home in Salt Lake for more than seven years.

Then, I was surprised to be called on another mission—I didn't think that happened. I was called as a health missionary to the Philippines! It was like the millennium to be back after eight years! This was the beginning (or deepening) of my "magnificent obsession": Church welfare and caring for the poor and the needy—and establishing Zion. Toward the end of that mission, I was sent to Hong Kong for a month to help the first health missionaries get started. When I returned to the Philippines, I was invited over the phone to work for the Church as coordinator of health missionaries and did that for close to three years. I learned much that helped determine my sense of direction for the years ahead.

Then—big surprise—I was called on another mission. I cried. I was thirty-six and had not been home quite three years from the last one. But I knew it was right. I knew God wanted me to go. In 1976, I found myself in Djakarta, Indonesia. My companion and I were the first lady missionaries and the first welfare missionaries to Indonesia. We spent two months at the brand new LTM in Provo learning the language (since she was a native of Malaysia, she already knew the language). I returned home in 1978, having spent a total of five years in Southeast Asia, my "second home."

Next I was asked to work at the LTM (now MTC), coordinating the training of welfare missionaries (formerly known as health missionaries). I became associate director of special training and was there for six years. During that time my favorite opportunity was teaching the "Sisters' Meeting" each Sunday. What a blessing that has been in my life! I have never enjoyed a church calling more.

In 1981, I had a chance to return to Asia for five weeks, going first to Thailand, where I visited my first refugee camp (later the Church made a video of one of my experiences there). Next I went to

Singapore, Indonesia, the Philippines, Hong Kong, and finally Taiwan. I worked with missionaries, visited friends, and got stuck in a hospital in Taipei! This was my first time as a patient! Exhaustion, plus Bangkok Flu. I made the trip home in a wheelchair.

Just when I thought I was "home to stay," another call—Africa. More tears. But again it was the right thing to do, so I went. Things which seem so hard often turn out to be some of our most important lessons. I served as director of the Thrasher International Program for Children, spending about six months (on three different trips) in Nigeria, working on a family-centered health and self-reliance project. Unfortunately, I became seriously ill and had to be sent back to the United States. I was hospitalized for a while and then spent three months gaining back my strength.

In 1985 I traveled to Geneva, Switzerland, for World Health Organization meetings. What a fascinating experience! My companion, Ann Laemmlen, and I had a chance to roam around for about a week after the meetings were finished. I was thankful for this opportunity since both my grandmothers were born in Switzerland. I had a sense of belonging that is hard to describe.

I returned to work at the MTC during the summer of 1985 and became associate director of training, working with missionaries with additional assignments—senior missionaries, mostly, but also young sisters who worked with welfare or in visitor centers.

The next big surprise in my life came in February of 1986 when I was called to be a member of the Relief Society General Board under the leadership of Barbara W. Winder. When I was set apart, Elder Goaslind blessed me with good health. The blessing came instantly. The very next day I was able to work an entire day for the first time since returning from Africa. I felt like singing hymns again, and I have had sufficient energy for almost all I have needed to do since that blessing.

During 1992 my position and responsibilities at the MTC changed. I was made a director of training for Asian languages and welfare missionaries. With my retirement in 1995, I will have served for thirty-three years in some aspect of missionary work.

I am a single woman who lives alone and who is mostly optimistic, generally happy, often silly, frequently weepy, and *never* bored. I am filled with memories and dreams, a lot of unanswered questions, and a lot of hope. I love life, gospel principles, people, water, scriptures, teaching, sports, reading, writing, children, happiness, and the "still small voice." I trust my Heavenly Father with all my heart.

I love autumn and Christmas. I can't stand contention or unkindness. I love to work, laugh, breathe, cry, teach, and spend time with people I love. I enjoy cleanliness, order, rain, orange juice, BYU football games, good music, pigs, and elephants. And I love to laugh and help make others happy.

I am surrounded by abundant blessings and have many reasons to be content and happy. I know that God lives and that Jesus is the Christ and my Savior and Redeemer. My goal is like that expressed by Enos—that some day I might "see His face with pleasure," knowing I have done the very best I could in all he has asked.

Mary Bee Jensen
International Folk Dancers

by

Susanne J. Davis,
Delynne B. Peay, and Marian W. Jensen

"Mary Bee," as she is affectionately known, has been called the "Challenger" and the "Dreamer of Dreams." Many have referred to her leadership of the folk dancers as "The Mary Bee Finishing School." Other comments: "She never left you where she found you," and, "She makes you into your best self, as a dancer and as a person. What she expects of you, you give." Obviously, Mary Bee's students saw in her example great strength in the areas of performance, success, and etiquette.

*W*hen a visitor once strolled through the office of Mary Bee Jensen, former artistic director of the BYU International Folk Dancers, he saw pinned to the bulletin board the statement: "The impossible we do at once. Miracles take a little longer." The impossible did indeed become possible under Mary's direction, and miracles even happened.

The Brigham Young University philosophy of "The World is Our Campus" became the standing International Folk Dance slogan—a slogan that made students from many cultures feel at home in the program. With the incredible diversity and demands of this group, Mary Bee's ability to integrate, organize, and administrate became legendary. And her gift of creativity was what infused the program with its remarkable vitality. Nothing was ever impossible.

Mary's desire to provide others with opportunities for growth and accomplishment began at a young age. In 1934, a Provo, Utah, women's club selected Mary Bee, a student at Provo High School, as the all-around outstanding girl at the school. The medal was awarded on the basis of scholarship, service, and athletics. From this experience, a life-long passion developed. Mary wanted others to have memorable accomplishments in life, a desire that has clearly been fulfilled in her countless BYU folk-dance performances throughout the world.

Her unfailing enthusiasm and concern for others result perhaps most from her upbringing. Mary Bee was born in Provo, Utah, to Robert George and Mary Cuthbertson Bee. Her father, a scientist, was especially energetic, and her caring mother provided an environment of love. Mary grew up with three brothers. In their Protestant home, the parents stressed ethical standards and cultivated an interest in the arts and other intellectual matters. As a child, Mary learned to love fine music—her father played the cello and her mother was an accomplished pianist. Mary also learned to play the piano well and still plays for her own enjoyment. Occasionally, she also still plays duets with her brothers.

After graduating from high school, she attended Park College, a small private college in Parkville, Missouri, where she received her B.S. degree in biology. During her summers she was regularly employed at YWCA camps in Colorado. She loved the grandeur and beauty of nature.

It was not until 1940, when she was teaching at Jordan High School in Salt Lake Valley, that she met a young man who suited her fancy. It was a whirlwind courtship—after six weeks of dating, Mary Bee and Don A. Jensen were married. They have two sons, Don Bee and James R. Jensen, both of whom are currently married and raising families with the same passion for life characteristic of their mother.

Mary joined the Brigham Young University Physical Education Department in 1952 and taught an array of classes: soccer, hockey, tumbling, softball, and badminton. She even helped develop the first precision marching group, the Cougarettes. But in 1956, Mary and Don decided to make some changes. With contract in hand, they were on their way to the University of Santa Barbara, where Mary would start teaching that fall. Before they left, however, she provided some Scandinavian dances for a local Orem ward program. Watching that performance were two BYU faculty members, Dr. Harvey Taylor and Dr. Leona Holbrook. They were so impressed with the performance that they went to President Ernest Wilkinson to ask him to persuade Mary to stay at BYU. Thus began her long and successful career with the BYU International Folk Dancers.

The original folk-dance group consisted of six couples. But it soon grew at an astonishing rate to over three-hundred members. The group's local tours expanded to tours around the world as it became more professional. The folk dancers performed at the Lincoln Center, Carnegie Hall, Disneyland, and the Trocadero in Paris. And with time, Mary Bee's dancers earned the respect of professional dance groups in Europe. They have since danced before royalty and many leading dignitaries in Denmark, Spain, England, and the Philippines. The tours have taken the renowned group to eastern and western Europe, Asia, and the Middle East. And along the way, the dancers made new friends for the United States and for the Church. Under Mary Bee's leadership, groups dancing at international festivals have appeared on the national television networks of Russia, Bulgaria, Poland, Turkey, Israel, Austria, Belgium, Portugal, Japan, China, and the Philippines.

The tours were always well organized. Before leaving the United States, Mary Bee reminded her groups that they officially represented BYU and the Church and thus were to adhere to all the standards of both institutions. If they didn't, they would be sent home. No doubt Mary Bee would have followed through if she had had reason.

While Mary Bee was the artistic director, the group's tour manager was frequently her husband, Don Jensen. Accompanying them were always three or four musicians and several chaperones—faculty members or, at times, BYU administrators, including President Ernest Wilkinson, President Jeffrey Holland, and President Harvey Taylor. General Authorities have also accompanied them, including Elder Howard W. Hunter, Elder Boyd K. Packer, and Elder Robert L. Simpson.

Although Mary Bee is perhaps best known for these remarkable international tours, she will certainly never be forgotten at home. The annual performances of the BYU dance concert, Christmas Around the World, which she directed for twenty-six years, have become a Christmas tradition for the entire BYU community. Mary Bee saw these concerts as a seasonal gift of love—a gift that would increase understanding for the peoples of the world.

At any BYU folk-dance performance, members of the audience find themselves captivated by the animated performers and the colorful, authentic costumes. Frequently the audience spontaneously begins clapping as the performers stomp, click, clog, or whirl to the rhythmic folk music from around the world. Occasionally, during a vigorous performance, a braid might come loose from the head of a Hungarian dancer, or a petticoat fall down. Somehow the performers always manage to recover from these mishaps and keep dancing. Perhaps a hat might fall or a shoe wiggle off, or even a bodice rip. But the show must go on, and it always does, as if nothing were amiss.

Mary Bee Jensen's tireless service with this talented group of dancers was not only recognized within the university setting, but was acknowledged by organizations on national and international levels. She served as a delegate to the World Congress Confederation of International Organizers for Folklore Festivals, where she was referred to as "Mrs. Folk Dance." Also on the international scene, she was a participant in the Arts Educators of America in Romania and Poland. Other recognitions included being listed in *Outstanding*

Educators of America and receiving the BYU Karl G. Maeser Distinguished Teacher Award, the BYU Outstanding Woman Award, the BYU Alumni Distinguished Service Award, and KSL's Outstanding Teacher Award. She also served on the Board of Trustees of Ballet West, Salt Lake City, Utah. And as a token of her outstanding service to the community, the mayor of Provo, Utah, proclaimed a "Mary Bee Jensen Day" during the 1970s.

After she had led the Folk Dance group for about twenty years, Mary's youngest son served an LDS mission. The crowning experience of Jimmy's mission was to baptize his own mother. Without fanfare, Mary Bee flew to her son's place of labor for the ordinance. She had lived according to the principles of the gospel all her life. When the baptism occurred, her family members quietly rejoiced.

Mary Bee did not retire from the folk dance program without leaving a generous gift—the creation of the first international folk-dance scholarship fund at BYU. This endowment provides funding for two students for an entire school year. They must demonstrate high-quality dance performance, academic excellence, discipline, and personal development. Having accomplished this last dream, Mary Bee Jensen retired from Brigham Young University and the International Folk Dancers in 1986—after thirty-three years of selfless giving.

BYU International Folk Dancers
1977 European Tour
by
Susan J. Kiser, former BYU folk dancer

In 1977, I traveled on a BYU folk-dance tour to Europe. We went as ambassadors of BYU, representing both the United States and the Church. We hoped to be an uplifting influence to members and nonmembers alike. Our team performed in six missions of the Church—the last was the Warsaw, Poland, Mission. Ten days before our arrival in Poland, President

Kimball had visited that land and had set Poland apart as a mission field for the Church. It was exciting to follow in his footsteps and try to help the missionary effort in our unique way.

On Monday morning, September 4, we left a festival in Fribourg, Switzerland, for a trip to Zakopane, Poland. Unlike the festival in Switzerland, the Polish festival would be a competition, where eight Polish mountain groups and fourteen other dance groups from various countries would be in attendance. We were the first Americans ever to compete there.

On Tuesday, September 5, 1977, our group crossed the border in a coal-powered train from free Vienna to Communist-ruled Czechoslovakia. Our train stopped in a border town called Breclaw. Suddenly an armed guard entered our train compartment and asked for our passports. When we showed them, he then demanded to see transit visas. We didn't have any because we had been told by authorities in the United States that visas weren't needed as long as we didn't disembark the train. The guard told us to pay for individual transit visas or he would disengage our part of the train and send us back to Vienna. Our tour manager, Don Shaw, a member of the Health Department faculty, was not allowed off the train to contact our embassy for help. Since we were already late for the festival and were given only twelve minutes to make the decision, Professor Shaw handed over $477 for our transit visas. When he requested a receipt, the guard retorted "Your stamped passport is your receipt!" It was easy to determine where the money went: those border guards got an illegal bonus that day. That was our introduction to a communist country.

Late that night, when we arrived in Zakopane, Poland, we learned our luggage and costumes had not arrived with us. We had already been in our travel clothes for thirty-six hours, so we figured a few more wouldn't hurt. However, the situation became more tense the next day when our scheduled performance in front of the judges was just hours away and we still had no costumes, an important contributor to the authenticity and professionalism of our dances. Imagine, for instance, a clog dance without tap shoes.

Wednesday evening arrived and still no costumes. We said a prayer and prepared to perform in what we were wearing. Welcome news came a short time before the performance when the judges informed us they would allow us to perform again on Friday night and would delay judging until then.

When the announcer introduced us in Polish, he said, "Here come the Americans without their clothes on!" The audience roared. As a group we pulled together and put on one of our best shows of the tour. It was rewarded by a standing ovation at the end.

An added highlight was discovering that the Church's only missionary couple in Poland was in the audience. (They did not know the BYU folk dancers were scheduled to perform that night—just that an American group was to dance.) It was exciting to visit after the performance and realize we were not alone in our desires to do missionary work in that country. Brother Matthew W. Ciembronowicz was grateful for our appearance and suggested that our public-relations efforts would probably do more than what he and his wife would be able to do in the next six months.

Friday arrived. We still had not received any luggage or costumes. By that time we had lived in the same clothes for about five days and were starting to doubt that we would be able to perform in costume that evening for the judges. But miracles do happen. When we returned from a performance in Wadiwice, we found that our costumes had arrived at last. Evidently they had been impounded at the Czechoslovakian border—perhaps by the same border guard who had pocketed our money. That night we were able to dance in costume for the judges and give them our best effort.

The next day we were informed that we had swept the festival. We won in our division, our band was declared the best of the festival, and our violinist, Kelly Clark, was judged the best musician of the event. However, what meant the most to me was receiving the People's Prize as the superior group in the festival.

As I reflect back on that trip, I am impressed by what seems the work of Providence. The problems with our luggage turned to our advantage since we were able to perform for twice as many people as any other group and thus represent the Church to more than we could have done otherwise. I also like to think that having Poland's only missionary couple in the audience was not coincidental.

Jane "Janie" Thompson

Director of BYU's Program Bureau, Young Ambassadors, and Lamanite Generation

by

Shaunna Erwin

Director of BYU's Program Bureau and founder/director of the Young Ambassadors and Lamanite Generation, Janie Thompson has toured the world spreading gospel values. In all her entertainment work, she has emphasized the importance of high moral standards.

I don't mean to scare you, but I won't put my shows on for this audience. These men are too vulgar," warned the Special Services Director at a Marine base in the Orient. It was the summer of 1960 and Jane Thompson, better known as "Janie," was on her first overseas tour with the Program Bureau of BYU. Janie peered out at the rowdy crowd of Marines. "They're just young people like you. Let's do our show and have a good time," Janie said to encourage her suddenly apprehensive students. Janie's words were enough. The talented members of the Program Bureau ran on stage shouting the name of their show, "Curtain Time, Curtain Time, Curtain Time!"

"Those Marines turned out to be one of our favorite audiences," smiles Janie as she recalls the event. "They laughed, cheered, clapped, and responded with such enthusiasm that we couldn't help but do our best. We always had a rousing patriotic finish that brought them to their feet night after night."

So, just how did Janie do it?

"When many other U.S. campuses were facing problems with rebellious students, and when already declining moral values were almost dropping out of existence, the majority of our students were holding firm," writes Janie in her chapter of an unpublished family history. "The Program Bureau members caught the vision and were not afraid to buck the trend of the world as we prepared and performed for people in ever-widening areas of the country. We had flashy but modest costumes, exciting but nonsuggestive dance routines, and catchy but wholesome lyrics. And the comedy acts were screamingly funny without vulgarity. It wasn't easy, but those were our goals, and we stuck to them!"

Janie was born August 20, 1921, in Malta, Idaho, to John Henry and Lora Harmon Thompson. During World War II, she was a music student at BYU, and after graduation in 1943, she began teaching fifth-grade music at Timpanogos Elementary School in Provo. It was then that she was asked to sing with a band put together by a group of Army engineers. When she declined, they asked another girl. "That cut to the quick," Janie recalls. "She was everything I wasn't. She was beautiful. She was popular. And besides that, she could play the piano better than I could." Janie's jealousy got the best of her, and she decided she wanted to sing with them after all.

Janie left Utah and headed to California to get some entertainment experience. As she drove through Las Vegas, she saw that the Army band was playing. Janie immediately stopped the car and the next thing she knew she was singing "Someday He'll Come Along" with the band. After the show, someone told her she sounded like Ella Fitzgerald. "Of course I didn't really sound like Ella Fitzgerald, but that's all I needed to hear. From then on you couldn't shut me up."

Maybe you couldn't shut Janie up, but you surely could change the direction of her voice. She left the spotlight in 1950 when she was called on an LDS mission to Great Britain, or "just to Wales" as she puts it (she was never transferred). While serving as a missionary, Janie started a branch chorus, a district chorus, a Relief Society chorus, an MIA chorus, a Primary chorus, and even a priesthood chorus.

Upon returning to the States, Janie decided she wanted to rejoin Ike Carpenter's band—she had sung with them before her mission. She could hardly wait to perform in the big ballrooms of California once again. But before Janie even unpacked her suitcase in Los Angeles, her telephone rang. It was W. Cleon Skousen, head of public relations at Brigham Young University, calling on behalf of President Ernest L. Wilkinson to offer Janie a position as director of the BYU Program Bureau. "My heart sank; it really did. I didn't have any desire to work at BYU because it wasn't in my plan. But somehow I knew I should accept. Anything to do with the Church or BYU was sort of life-or-death to me. You just don't turn down those callings." So Janie headed back to Provo, crying all the way.

The Program Bureau was a student organization that had existed for many years before Janie was hired to lead it. But once Janie arrived, the program took on new meaning. Its primary function had been to serve the surrounding communities by filling requests for student talent features. This gave the students opportunities to develop and use their abilities in new realms. When Brother Skousen heard about Janie's successes, he attended a show and decided such shows would be useful to the university's public relations. Janie was then chosen to direct the new effort.

Janie didn't take her new position lightly—she didn't know the meaning of lightly. Given a small office in the Karl G. Maeser building, Janie began to make do with whatever space she could find. "Just finding rehearsal space was a huge challenge—I had to be creative. Many a time I pushed that old upright piano in the Social Hall into the ladies room—when the custodians weren't looking—and held girl-rehearsals in there!"

But Janie was used to finding odd places to rehearse. Every Wednesday night when she was a young girl, the movies came to her hometown. "Oh how I anticipated those shows," says Janie. "But sometimes I loved something else even better—my chance to stay home alone! I would push back the tables and chairs in the living room, turn up the radio, then dance and dance, making up the most incredible routines my lively imagination could come up with. I just knew there was a talent scout watching me through every crack in the walls, and there were lots of cracks!" Although the talent scouts never showed up at one of her living-room rehearsals, her talent was blooming nonetheless. Still blooming many years later, Janie's talent found especially fertile ground at BYU.

After Janie's experience in front of the Marines on her first overseas tour with the Program Bureau, those tours became "a way of life." Between 1962 and 1969, the group traveled to Europe, Greenland, Iceland, Newfoundland, Labrador, the Orient, the Caribbean, and the Middle East.

In 1970, a co-worker said, "Janie, sometime we should name a show-group 'Ambassadors,' because that is what we really are." Janie responded, "Yes, and they should be called 'Young Ambassadors' with the name 'Young' standing for Brigham Young." After a request from Japan for BYU to represent American universities at the World's Fair in Osaka, Japan, the Young Ambassadors were born. Janie stayed with that group for two years, traveling to Europe, India, Sri Lanka, and Nepal.

But even with the success of the Program Bureau and the Young Ambassadors, Janie was trying to put another group together. She wanted to create a show featuring the Lamanite culture. In 1971, President Dale Tingey of the Southwest Indian Mission asked for help in building an all-Lamanite show to stimulate missionary work. That was the beginning of the Lamanite Generation. "At first it was not a BYU show, but a mission show," recalls Janie. "I helped, because I was curious to see if I really could do anything with the Lamanites—I like to think that the Lord's fingers were at my back. From very humble beginnings (we had to ride in the back of trucks, sleep on floors, and swelter in the Arizona heat—our only air-conditioning was opening the window) it has grown into one of the most unique and important performing groups in existence."

Now retired, Janie sits in her office, walls covered with pictures of students. She repeats two truths about show business. "First: it is a powerful and influential teacher—a great big visual aid. And if we don't know how powerful and influential it is, there is someone else who does. The adversary uses it to full advantage to encourage immorality, immodesty, the breakup of the home and family, violence, crime, the use of alcohol, drugs, and tobacco, and all that so-called 'good stuff.' The sad truth is that most of us sit around and let him get away with it. Second: you can sell a product with a song and a dance. This is proven to us daily—it works. They are called commercials."

Janie always remembered her two truths in every performance, no matter where her groups were performing. She believes in the power of the Spirit and the influence it can have in others' lives. "I feel we have important products to sell and we should be using the media and our talents to advertise what our Church stands for—clean living, happiness, and holding to worthwhile values." Janie is now writing about her experiences with the Program Bureau, Young Ambassadors, and the Lamanite Generation, and is busy checking out the missionary results of their shows.

She may have been named just plain Jane, but Janie's accomplishments are anything but plain. Jayne B. Malan, author of the article "Janie Thompson—She's 'been everywhere' spreading the message of love and brotherhood" (March 1986 *Ensign*, p. 36), notes that Janie "never mentions her role in the blessings received by her students. She doesn't seem to realize the impact she has had on their lives and the strength they receive because she lets them know, without question, that they can count on her. She tells them. They sing about it in 'Count on Me,' a song she wrote for the Lamanite Generation and she lives her life accordingly:

> You know if you need me I'll be there.
>
> I'll go anywhere.
>
> Hope then you'll see
>
> That you can always count on me . . .
>
> I will understand.
>
> Eternally, count on me."

Artemesia Romney Ballif

Friend and Supporter

by

Bonnie Ballif-Spanvill and Heather Bennet Hanson

In 1993 Arta Ballif passed away after a life of amazing productivity. Her youngest daughter, Bonnie, and a granddaughter, Heather, provide an insightful portrait of a woman whose creative accomplishments represent a lifetime of loyalty to family, church, and Brigham Young University.

*A*rtemesia Romney Ballif pursued life with an artist's eye, a learner's mind, and a loving spirit. Arta was known for her love, her faith, her desire to achieve, her creative pursuit of all that is beautiful and true, and her fierce attachment to the promise of each day.

She was born on August 27, 1904, in Colonia Juarez, Chihuahua, Mexico, to George Samuel and Artemesia Redd Romney as their fifth of ten children. After becoming refugees of the 1912 Mexican Civil War, her family traveled from El Paso, Texas, to Los Angeles, to Salt Lake City, and finally settled in Rexburg, Idaho, where her father became president of Ricks College.

Her love of theater began in childhood. She acted in and directed many plays and eventually received the Jon Green Award for distinguished service in the dramatic arts from the Utah Valley Theater Guild in 1987. Arta wrote and delivered countless programs for various clubs and organizations, lectured for Brigham Young University's continuing education program throughout the western states, and wrote essays and conducted interviews for her own radio show, "Challenge to Thought," on KOVO.

Along with her gifts in drama, Arta found equal success in her writing. She published short stories, poetry, and children's stories in magazines and newspapers. She won awards from the Utah Arts Council and in the BYU Literature and Christian Values contest. The Babcock Reading Arts Society and the BYU English Department have both featured her poetry. Three books contain her writings and illustrations: *The World and I, Lamentations,* and *Pieces of Glee from Inside of Me.*

Throughout her life Arta expressed her talent as a visual artist through painting, needlework, home decoration, and the fashions she created for herself and her family. In her later years, she studied painting privately and completed hundreds of works from miniature oils to the expansive sky-and-cloud canvases that became her passion in the late 1980s. She was honored with eight one-woman shows and with an award from the American Artists Professional League. Dozens of her paintings are in private collections around the world.

Her education did not end when she graduated with high honors from Ricks College in 1925; education became a life-long pursuit for Arta. When all her children were in school, she returned to finish her bachelor's degree in English and theater arts at Brigham Young University. She received it with highest honors in 1953 and earned a master's degree from BYU two years later, also with honors.

Arta blessed her family with her creative talents and pursuit of learning. Just two years after she married Ariel Smith Ballif in the Salt Lake Temple in 1925, Arta was called with her husband to serve a mission in New Zealand. While he was principal of the LDS Maori Agricultural College, she organized fifty-two Primaries throughout the mission and wrote the lessons given in them.

In 1930 they returned to Idaho where Ariel taught at Midway High School. Then, during the Depression, they sold their possessions and took their children to Los Angeles, where Ariel pursued graduate studies at the University of Southern California. In 1939, he came to teach in the Department of Sociology at Brigham Young University, and for a significant period of that time was the department chair. All the while, Arta sought out beauty and understanding. She made her home a gracious refuge for her husband and five children, even when resources were limited.

Arta and Ariel were called again to New Zealand in 1955 to preside over the LDS mission there. Under their stewardship, a stake was organized and a college and temple were built and dedicated. Arta served as mission mother and made a major contribution to the development of the Church auxiliaries there.

During more than sixty-seven years of marriage, Arta and Ariel shared a broad range of experience, from traveling around the world to working side by side in their garden. When Ariel was not teaching, caring for his family, working in Church callings, or in his garden, he loved to sing with a BYU quartet. His rich tenor voice was a definite asset to this popular musical group, which included Ralph Britsch, Lee Valentine, Fred Webb, Leland Perry, and others, as changes were needed. Arta loved to hear him sing and wished that she had one other talent—the ability to accompany her husband on the piano. This perhaps was the only ability she lacked.

Their influence on each other was both positive and profound. BYU gave a Distinguished Alumni Award to each of them, and in 1988, they were awarded a Presidential Citation for their civic, professional, and religious accomplishments.

Beyond her missionary service, Arta contributed to The Church of Jesus Christ of Latter-day Saints as president of the Rigby Stake Young Women's Mutual, president of the BYU Stake Relief Society, a member of the Sunday School General Board, a member of the family home evening manual writing committee, and in various ward callings. She was also president of other organizations: the Player's Guild, the Literary League, and BYU Women.

During Arta's last few years, she developed a heart condition and her body began to weaken. Thus, she was restricted from some of her many activities. Although she was surrounded by children, grandchildren, and friends, she must have chafed because she was not able to help and mingle with them as she had in the past. When she passed away in 1993, she must have realized, as did all those who knew her, that her life had been filled with service and love.

Endnotes

Patricia Terry Holland

1 Holland, Jeffrey R, "Virtus et Veritas." *Brigham Young University 1981–82 Fireside and Devotional Speeches* (Provo, UT: University Publications, 1982), 7.

2 Holland, Jeffrey R. and Patricia T, "Some Things We Have Learned—Together." *Brigham Young University 1984–85 Devotional and Fireside Speeches* (Provo, UT: University Publications, 1985), 62–63.

3 Bell, James P., "An Apostolic Call." *Brigham Young Magazine* 48, no. 3 (August 1994): 23–25.

Janet Griffin Lee

1 Lee, Rex and Janet, with Jim Bell, *Marathon of Faith* (Salt Lake City: Deseret Book, 1996), 6.

Susan Elizabeth Howe

1 Howe, Susan Elizabeth, "Getting Somewhere." in *Women Steadfast in Christ*, ed. Dawn Hall Anderson and Marie Cornwall (Salt Lake City: Deseret Book, 1992), 224.

2 Jenkins, Carri P., "A Closer Look: Susan E. Howe, Assistant Professor of English," *Brigham Young Magazine* 47, no. 3 (August 1993): 18.

3 Jenkins, 18.

4 Jenkins, 18.

5 Jenkins, 19.

7 Jenkins, 19.

8 Howe, 223–25.

9 Howe, 230.

Index